LIFE IN ANCIENT GREECE

Reader's
Digest

Published by

THE READER'S DIGEST ASSOCIATION LIMITED

London New York Sydney
Montreal Cape Town

JOURNEYS INTO THE PAST

LIFE IN ANCIENT GREECE

TAKING A STAND
The javelin was used in war and for hunting as well as in sport.

ELITIST SPORT Only the very rich could afford horses which they raced bareback – or had slaves to race for them – or rode in the cavalry.

GETTING A GRIP
Heads down and arms extended, wrestlers prepare for the throw.

LIFE IN ANCIENT GREECE
Edited and designed by Toucan Books Limited
Sole author: Sophia Sackville-West

First edition copyright © 1997
The Reader's Digest Association Limited
11 Westferry Circus, Canary Wharf,
London E14 4HE

Copyright © 1996
Reader's Digest Association Far East Limited
Philippines copyright © 1996
Reader's Digest Association Far East Limited
All rights reserved

® Reader's Digest, The Digest and the Pegasus logo are registered trademarks of The Reader's Digest Association, Inc, of Pleasantville, New York, USA

Printing and binding: Printer Industria Gráfica S.A., Barcelona
Separations: Litho Origination, London
Paper: Smurfit Condat, Neuilly, France

ISBN 0 276 42129 9

Front cover (clockwise from top left): Painting figurines; view of Delphi; young girl washing, detail from drinking cup; nurse bringing child to its mother, vase detail; Hellenistic silver bowl; hunter; girl with doves, from tomb relief.

Back cover (clockwise from top left): Treasury House, Delphi; view of Athens, painted 1830; a healing sanctuary, from votive relief; artists painting the frieze on the Parthenon; vase detail showing Delphic oracle.

PAGE 1 The god Apollo, patron of music, clutches a tortoiseshell lyre. The crow – believed to be oracular – was often associated with him.

PAGES 2 AND 3 A wedding procession makes its way to the groom's house on a 6th-century BC Attic vase.

CONTENTS

DIVINE CLOTHES
The goddess
Hera's cloak and
gown are also
typical dress for
mortals.

**SACRED SPOT Ruins at
Corinth stand against a
mountain background.**

**REFLECTING AN AGE A mid
5th-century BC bronze
mirror is mounted on a
female figure.**

**IN THE SWING A vase
shows a woman
sitting on a swing
between two men.**

TAKING A BREAK
While men
reclined,
women usually
sat on stools
or chairs.

WHO WERE THE GREEKS?

The cultural flowering of ancient Greece was crammed into 400 years from the late

8th century BC to the early 4th. During that time a handful of thinkers and artists created works of

astonishing sophistication. The majority of Greeks, however, remained hard-working peasants.

FOR THE Athenian statesman Pericles in the 5th century BC, it was a combination of intense patriotism and muscular idealism that made his city great. In a funeral speech, recorded by the historian Thucydides, to commemorate those who had died in the first year of the Peloponnesian War against Sparta (431-404 BC), he drew a compelling – if heavily idealised – picture of life in Athens at the peak of its glory:

'Our constitution is named a democracy because it is in the hands not of the few, but of the many . . . And as we give free play to all in our public life, so we carry the same spirit into our daily relations with one another. We have no black looks nor angry words for our neighbour if he enjoys himself in his own way, and we abstain from little acts of churlishness which, though they leave no mark, yet cause annoyance to whosoever notes them. Open and friendly in our private intercourse, in our public acts we keep strictly within the control of the law. We acknowledge the restraint of reverence; we are obedient to whosoever is set in authority . . . We are lovers of beauty without extravagance, and lovers of wisdom without unmanliness.'

The Greek way of life, especially that of Pericles' Athens, has had admirers ever since. But the classical Greece of the 5th and early 4th centuries BC, although it had highly advanced forerunners in the

ANTECEDENT CIVILISATION This Minoan fresco from Knossos in Crete dates from around 1400 BC.

eastern Mediterranean such as the Minoans of Crete, had mostly evolved from a primitive society. This extended its ribald and superstitious fingers from the dark ages of prehistory into the lives of even the most sophisticated citizens of classical Athens – about whom we know more than about the people of any other Greek society. Moreover, Athens, in the view not least of its own inhabitants, was untypically 'civilised'. Its great rival Sparta in the Peloponnese, as described by many Athenians, was an illiterate, militaristic, totalitarian regime.

Indeed, the majority of Greeks, even in 5th-century BC Attica, whose centre was Athens, were peasants, eking out a precarious existence from small plots of fertile land amid a landscape that was often too mountainous for extensive agriculture. Unlike the Romans, the Greeks made virtually no advances on their original farming methods – nor did they devise much else of lasting technological utility. They worked hard from spring to autumn and spent the idle winter months worrying that their food stores might run out.

Peasants found release from the harshness of
continued on page 10

DANGER AT SEA Treacherous currents and rocky shorelines – such as the coast of Cephalonia here – made life hazardous for Greek seafarers.

45°

5°   10°   15°   20°

Massilia○   ○ Nicaea
              Antipolis

40°

○ Rome

M

e

d

Taras
Elea○   ○Sybaris

i   Croton○

t   Strait of
       Messina

e   *Sicily* ○Naxos
              Leontini○
r   Syracuse○

r

a

n

e

a

n

THESSALY   *Aegean*

Pharsalus○

Thermopylae

PHOCIS   Elateia   EUBOEA
Cephissus Lake
Ithaca   *Copais*   Chalcis○
Delphi○   BOEOTIA   Delium○ Acharnae
          Thebes○   ○Rhamnus
Corinthian Gulf Plataea○ Mt Parnes ○
ACHAEA Pallene   Eleusis○ Marathon○
                    Athens○
Sicyon○   Megara○ Piraeus○
Elis○   Nemaea○ Corinth○ *Salamis* ATTICA
Olympia○ Mantinea○ Mycenae○ *Saronic Gulf*
              Argos○ Epidaurus○ *Aegina* ○ *Mt Laurium*
          Tegea○
Peloponnese
MESSENIA Sparta○
Taÿgetos Mts *Eurotas* LACONIA

Mediterranean Sea

0   100 km
0   50 miles

20°

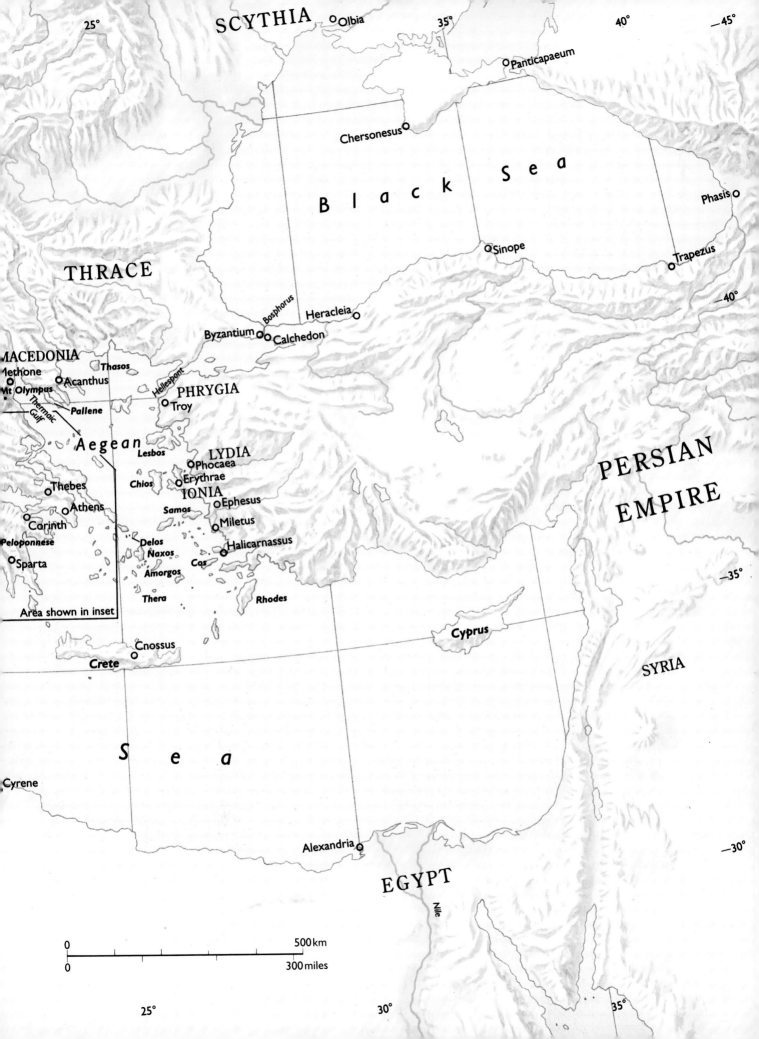

SCYTHIA

○ Olbia

○ Panticapaeum

Chersonesus ○

B l a c k   S e a

Phasis ○

○ Sinope

Trapezus ○

THRACE

Heracleia ○

Byzantium ○ ○ Calchedon

Bosphorus

Hellespont

MACEDONIA

Methone

○ Acanthus

Thasos

Mt Olympus

Thermaic Gulf

Pallene

PHRYGIA

○ Troy

Aegean

Lesbos

LYDIA

○ Phocaea

Chios

○ Erythrae

IONIA

Thebes ○

○ Ephesus

Samos

Athens ○

○ Miletus

Corinth ○

Delos

○ Halicarnassus

Peloponnese

Naxos

Cos

○ Sparta

Amorgos

Thera

Rhodes

PERSIAN

EMPIRE

Area shown in inset

Cyprus

SYRIA

Cnossus ○

Crete

S e a

Cyrene

Alexandria ○

EGYPT

Nile

0   500 km

0   300 miles

their lives in the frequently oafish bacchanalias that enlivened village existence. They also sought comfort from a plethora of gods, nymphs and other supernatural beings. For the most part, they were only dimly aware of the intellectual or artistic achievements of their contemporaries. Some might have trudged in to attend the dramatic festivals held in cities such as Athens. Even so, many country people may not have seen any of the tragedies or comedies by Aeschylus, Aristophanes and their fellows for which classical Greece is now famous.

The intellectual achievements that ancient Greece bequeathed to later civilisations were the work, in fact, of a handful of upper-class thinkers who had the leisure for such pursuits. What was remarkable was their vigorous independence of mind – a self-confident questioning of everything around them that extended as far as the supernatural framework upon which Greek life was believed to rest.

One reason for the Greek achievement lay in a competitively extrovert spirit intolerant of both introspection and mediocrity. Conscious of a natural tendency to excess, Greek males exerted an intense self-discipline in their efforts to outdo their rivals in whatever field. Another secret of their success was the ability to assimilate foreign ideas and improve on them. Thus they borrowed from Egypt for their early sculpture; they were indebted to the Phoenicians of the eastern Mediterranean for the origin of their alphabet and to Babylon for their mathematics. Similarly, any indigenous gods discovered by Greek-speaking migrants were incorporated into an undogmatic and flexible set of

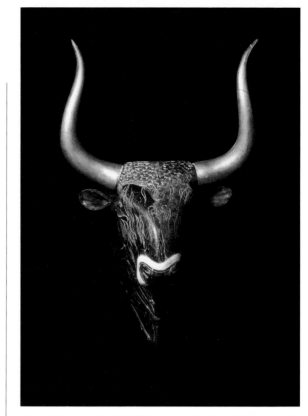

BULL'S HEAD   Crete's Minoan civilisation left its mark in the half-man, half-bull Minotaur of mythology.

religious beliefs that continued to make room for foreign newcomers throughout the classical era.

The glory of ancient Greece – lasting from the late 8th century to the early 4th century BC – can also be explained by its geography. Small plains interspersed a barren mountainous terrain and only 30 per cent of the land was cultivable. Land shortages made it necessary to found colonies to help to support the growing population; by the 5th century there were hundreds of Greek communities scattered around the Mediterranean and Black Sea – 'like frogs around a pond', in Plato's words. Poor roads and the natural barriers of mountains prevented easy land communication among the states so that

MULE TRAIN   The lame blacksmith god Hephaistus rides a mule. Mortals also used mules as load bearers.

THE BIRTH OF DEMOCRACY

THE TYRANTS who replaced the kings of Homer's Greece were not all tyrannical in the modern sense, and some even laid the foundations upon which democracy was later built. One example was the Athenian lawgiver Solon who in 594 BC abolished the system of debt bondage whereby the rich had reduced an entire class of the poor to serf status. From then onwards it was impossible to enslave a citizen for failing to repay debts – an enormous step forward in guaranteeing individual freedom.

Athens' second great lawgiver, Cleisthenes, brought democracy a step closer in 508-507 when he established the principle of equality under the law. But, although this was a radical departure, it remained an ideal to be striven for rather than a constitutional change. The word democracy was not coined until a generation later, and even in the golden age of Athenian democracy the *demos* or 'common people' did not include women, children, non-citizens or, of course, slaves.

The golden age came after the defeat of the Persians in the mid-5th century BC when ordinary Athenians began to demand a share in the fruits of their imperial success – aware that they were the ones who rowed the boats upon which the city's supremacy depended. In 462-461 Pericles in conjunction with the political leader Ephialtes launched an attack on the aristocratic power base, the Council of Areopagus. The principle of one man one vote assumed its purest form in the Assembly, which had always existed but increased in importance after the demise of the Areopagus. Here, all Athenian citizens had the right to cast their votes: in this respect Greek democracy differed from modern models in which we delegate decision-making to elected representatives.

Henceforth, Athenian government had to be seen to be conducted by and for the people.

Since it was mostly people out of sympathy with democracy who wrote about it there is little testimony to its ideal. Nevertheless, the majority of Athenians and many other Greeks believed firmly that only democracy could ensure their individual freedoms and equality before the law. Whenever faction (*stasis*) rent their society, the city became electrified with rumours of threatened tyranny. As a character in Aristophanes' *The Wasps* puts it: 'I have never heard the word "tyranny" in the last 50 years, but now it is cheaper than dried cod; just look how its name is bandied about in the Agora [market]. If a man is buying anchovies and does not want sardines, at once the man who is selling sardines nearby says: "This fellow seems like a man buying luxuries, with a view to tyranny." '

people travelled by sea in the more clement summer and stayed at home during the winter months. All this played its part in generating a bullish individualism in the inhabitants of the different communities. This, in its turn, prevented the formation of an all-Greek government and promoted constant warfare among the city-states. From 497 to 338 BC Athens was at war for three years out of every four. Only against the Persians in 490 and 480-479 BC were the Greeks able to unite effectively.

WHERE DID THE GREEKS COME FROM?

The Greeks first entered the territory now associated with them in about 2000 BC when Egypt was a great power and the Minoans of Crete were evolving a highly sophisticated society on their island. Modern scholars conjecture that some of these migrants, probably from the steppes of modern Russia and central Asia, moved to the mountainous north of modern Greece from where they re-emerged as the Dorian invaders of southern Greece seven centuries later. The rest are believed to have passed on to Thessaly and the south where 400 years later, in about 1600 BC, they created the sumptuous society of Mycenae in the Peloponnese.

Mycenae, later described by the poet Homer as 'rich in gold', prospered from trading ventures extending from southern Italy to the Syrian coast. It probably had sovereignty over other communities dotted around the Greek mainland, each of them centred on a royal palace. It was a busily bureaucratic and hierarchical society in which power devolved from king to feudal lord to villager and slave. After the Englishman Michael Ventris deciphered its 'Linear B' script in 1952, archaeologists discovered records of an enormous labour force made up of slaves and variously 'free' dependants, all with carefully differentiated jobs.

In about 1200 BC, the Mycenaean age ended catastrophically: palaces were set on fire, the administration collapsed and a 'dark age' descended on ancient Greece. Scholars still dispute the causes of this demise. Some believe there may have been a series of disastrous droughts, bringing famine in their train; others have speculated that civil strife or even raids by pirates may have been to blame. Another possible cause was invasion from the north, with the Dorians as likely invaders. Certainly, by the time communications among the Greek communities had been re-established in the 8th century, the Dorians had arrived in central and southern Greece from their northern fastnesses. Numerous city-states were sprouting up in mainland Greece, and others were being spawned on the islands of the Aegean and even farther afield.

By this time the Greeks had developed some sense of nationhood based on a common language and the worship of common gods. These enabled them to differentiate themselves from the non-Greek-speaking 'barbarians' living outside their lands. They called themselves the Hellenes and their nation Hellas, but they retained their hotch-potch of local dialects and insisted on parochial sovereignty.

GOD OF WINE Dionysus in a ship – for mortals, too, this was the best way of getting between the city-states.

The poet Homer provided a link between the early Mycenaean civilisation and this newly emerging Greek culture. He was composing his oral poetry around 700 BC after the migrations that followed the collapse of the Mycenaean culture. His two epic poems, the *Iliad* and the *Odyssey*, which described the heroic lives of kings and nobles in war and in peace, gave the Greeks their history, their gods and also their guidelines for living.

By the 8th century BC, the kings had largely disappeared and the nobles in many city-states had been divested of political power by coups d'état floated on popular unrest. The result was usually rule by 'tyrants' – some of whom were comparatively benevolent. The first 'age of the tyrants' (about 650-510 BC) coincided with the first written laws. Sparta alone retained two hereditary monarchs and a hierarchical militaristic government which existed somewhat anachronistically among the other city-states.

By this time the centre of power and wealth was Persia. In 545 BC the Persians conquered the Ionian Greek cities of the coast of Asia Minor, following this up with the subjection of Thrace and Macedonia. The Greeks smarted under foreign rule. In 490 the Athenians defeated a Persian force at Marathon; later, in a rare coordinated effort led by an Athenian-Spartan coalition, the Greeks defeated the Persians at Salamis in 480 and Plataea in 479, crowning their victories with the Peace of Callias in 449 BC. No one would have believed that this group of individualistic city-states could pool their resources to overcome the greatest power the world had seen.

The defeat of the Persians in 479 BC marks the beginning of the classical era and the Athenian Empire. The Confederacy of Delos had been founded to pursue the war against Persia, but after the

ROYAL HOMAGE **Princes from Crete (left) and the Aegean (right) pay tribute to an Egyptian ruler of about 1450 BC.**

Persian defeat Athens continued the 'alliance'. In effect, she subordinated the islands and states of the northern and eastern coasts of the Aegean to her sovereignty. She also exacted tribute from them which largely financed both her navy and Athenian freedom from internal taxation. Meanwhile, Sparta dominated most of the Peloponnese.

But peace among these irascible city-states was never long-term. The Peloponnesian War between Sparta and Athens was fought for domination of Greece. It lasted from 431 to 404 BC and ended with total Athenian defeat, the dissolution of her empire and the devastation of Attic countryside. This was the beginning of the end for the Athenians whose fighting spirit had been drained by the combined effects of the long, impoverishing years of war against Sparta, a great plague and a disastrous military-cum-naval expedition to Sicily which ended in Athenian rout in 413 BC.

But the final blow for Athens came from a previously despised state. In 359 BC, Philip II, whom the Athenian general Demosthenes dismissed as 'a lousy Macedonian', became king of this wild northern

continued on page 16

13

ATHENA'S SACRED CITY

THE PROCESSION that marked the highlight of the Panathenaea festival – held in mid-August – moves along Athens' only major thoroughfare, the Panathenaic Way, towards the Acropolis. It was always headed by young maidens (*kanephoroi*), followed by old men carrying branches and young men leading animals for sacrifice. Bringing up the rear were cavalrymen. With them the worshippers carried a robe, woven during the previous year by the women of Athens, for the much-venerated, wooden image of the goddess Athena kept in the Acropolis's Erechtheum.

On its way, the procession passed across the open space of the Agora (marketplace), overlooked by the temple of the blacksmith god Hephaestus (Hephaestion) perched on its hill. Almost opposite the main stairway leading up to the Acropolis rose the hill of Ares where the council of the Areopagus met and murder trials were held. Beyond that (to the right) was the hill of the Pnyx where the Athenian Assembly met.

HEAT OF THE BATTLE
A Roman mosaic shows Darius of Persia lunging out at Alexander the Great during the Battle of Issos in 333 BC.

tribe. He harnessed a mixture of intelligence and ruthlessness to a programme of conquest that subordinated all of Greece. In 334 his son Alexander the Great succeeded him and continued to conquer everything from Libya to Samarkand and Karachi before his followers called a halt at the Indus river. Shortly afterwards, in 332, Alexander died. During the subsequent Hellenistic age which lasted until eventual Roman conquest in 146 BC, Alexander's empire was divided among monarchies established by rival subordinates.

THE GREEK LEGACY
The classical age was over and with it the essence of Athenian glory. But Greek culture and government had been exported all over the near East and many of the new rulers were Greek. Egypt was ruled by a Greek dynasty for the next 300 years.

Even when Greece had become a province of the Romans, the eastern half of the empire continued to speak Greek and rich Roman youths flocked to the finishing school of the Athenian universities.

The Greeks have continued to influence the Western world – far more, in fact, than any other nation with the possible exception of the Jews. Greek as well as Jewish thought had a vital influence on early Christian preachers and thinkers including St Paul in the 1st century AD and St Augustine of Hippo in the 5th. Through them and others like them it helped to shape the whole course of European Christian civilisation.

This influence can be seen and felt all around us. To this day, cities are planned on a classical grid-pattern first used by Hippodamus of Miletus in the mid 5th century BC, while every porticoed bank or parliament building in Europe and the Americas and beyond owes its design to the ancient Greeks. Most modern European languages are infused with Greek words and most of our literary forms were bequeathed by them. The Greeks invented history, biography, tragedy and democracy. And their insatiable curiosity – allied to a conviction that all knowledge is discoverable through sheer hard thought – has provided the inspiration as well as the framework for much subsequent intellectual endeavour.

CELESTIAL CITY Athens rises from the plain of Attica in a 19th-century aquatint by Edward Dodwell. The achievements of ancient Greece have haunted the imaginations of generations of Western artists and scholars.

THE LIFE CYCLE IN GREECE

Men and women sought the goodwill of the gods through religious ritual
at all the important turning points in life. Rich families, like the one above,
could sometimes afford to sacrifice an animal at home; poorer citizens
made do with vegetarian offerings. The male head of the household
dominated proceedings, as he did every aspect of family life, but women,
children and household slaves all gathered for household worship.

WOMEN AND MEN

While the active and gregarious male was out working, talking or fighting, his wife was confined to

the home. Married off at the age of 15 to a 30-year-old man, her function was to bear legitimate

children – of whom the boys alone were eligible for citizenship – and run the house.

THE HISTORIAN and soldier Xenophon left a telling glimpse of domestic harmony in the home of one of Thebes' leading citizens, Leontiades. The context, however, was less than harmonious. The year was 379 BC during a period of factional infighting among the city-state's ruling class. One evening Phillidas, a leader of one of the factions, accompanied by three strong men came knocking on the door of Leontiades, whom Phillidas regarded as an enemy. 'Now it chanced that Leontiades had dined by himself and was still reclining on his couch after dinner, while his wife sat beside him, working with wool. And believing Phillidas to be trustworthy he bade him come in.' His trust was misplaced. With a ruthlessness almost worthy of 20th-century gangsters, Phillidas and his men entered the house, 'killed Leontiades and frightened his wife into silence. And as they went out, they ordered that the door should remain shut; and they

IMMACULATE CONCEPTION A 6th-century BC tripod (a vessel resting on three legs) shows the birth of the warrior goddess Athena from Zeus's head.

threatened that if they found it open, they would kill all who were in the house.'

Such bloody interruptions apart, home life for many women in ancient Greece, especially rich women, was a strictly sheltered affair, similar to that of their counterparts in some Islamic countries nowadays. Moments of shared domestic intimacy, such as that between Leontiades and his wife, may have been common enough in the privacy of families, but it would also have been well understood that the man's sphere and the woman's were quite separate – the man's lying outside the home, the woman's inside it. In the Athens of the 5th century BC, it was considered an outrage if a stranger entered a part of a house where women were present; they would immediately vanish to their segregated quarters. Poor women could enjoy meeting each other at the fountain, at work in the fields or as stallholders, but women of leisure had no such excuse,

---

WHERE IGNORANCE IS BLISS

CHILDHOOD IN THE shelter of their family homes was often a happy time for Greek girls. But marriage brought a sharp change of life, as Procne, in a play by the Athenian dramatist Sophocles, bemoans:
❝ Now outside [my family home] I am nothing. Yet I have frequently observed woman's nature in this regard, how we are nothing. When we are young in our father's house, I think we live the sweetest life of all humankind; for ignorance always brings children up delightfully. But when we have reached maturity and can understand, we are thrust out and sold away from the gods of our fathers and our parents, some to foreigners, some to barbarians, some to joyless houses, some full of reproach. And finally, once a single night has united us, we have to praise our lot and pretend that all is well. ❞

FAMILY PRIDE   Battling soldiers bear shields with their family crests on a vase from the 7th century BC.

since they had slaves to send on outside errands. As men did the shopping, women were left with little opportunity to venture beyond their own thresholds except on festival days. At home, the wife had complete dominion over the running of the household. But if her husband was less domestically inclined than the Theban Leontiades, she had little to entertain her when her principal tasks were over, apart from chatting with the other women of the household and indulging in daydreams as she carried on with her work at the loom and spindle.

Women lacked citizen status, and enjoyed only the most meagre rights in law. But since all the information we have about them comes from literature written by men, it is futile to speculate about their happiness. Some women were without doubt deeply loved and respected by their husbands – Aristotle, for example, was blissfully married and continually emphasised the virtues of matrimonial life.

Greek women had once, in fact, enjoyed a comparative freedom. Although the royal women in Homer's epics were all destined for marriage, they were portrayed out and about doing the washing and mixing with the men in the halls of their palaces. They were expected to be modest but they were not hidden away. Princesses such as Andromache and Helen wandered the streets of Troy with their escorts, and women are depicted on Achilles' shield helping to defend a city's walls.

It was the Athenian lawgiver Solon (*c.*640-560 BC) who limited the freedom of women as part of his extensive legislative programme: he laid down the walks they were allowed to take, their feasts, their mourning activities, what their trousseaux should consist of and even what they should eat and drink. Some of his reasons were economic – lavish funerals, trousseaux and feasts were typical of an aristocracy whose greed and ostentation was

GRIEF FOR A HERO One task ascribed to women was that of mourning the dead in suitable style. On this vase women are grieving over a fallen warrior.

causing civic unrest. But there were political reasons, too. With the coming of democracy, a different set of values, usually associated with the Athenian lower classes, came to predominate. According to these, the woman's role was definitely to be busy about domestic tasks.

CHOOSING A PARTNER

In Athens from about 500 BC, girls were married at the age of 15, often to men of around 30, who were chosen by their fathers or nearest male relation; many of these girls were grandmothers by the time they were 30. It was believed that a girl was most fertile at puberty, whereas an adolescent boy was considered to be at his least sexually productive age. A bride's virginity was essential, and to ensure that, daughters from rich households never went outside the house unaccompanied. The orator Xenophon stated that one wife had, until marriage, 'been closely supervised in order that she would see as little as possible, hear as little as possible and learn as little as possible'.

Generally speaking, daughters of rich and poor families alike married their kinsmen in order to consolidate the family's property and to ensure proper maintenance of the family burial plots (an

all-important duty); very occasionally half-brothers and half-sisters married each other. Many women were widowed before they were 20 as a result of the almost constant warfare waged by the Greeks. Although these women were expected and required to remarry, they were sometimes permitted to choose a second husband, and as a result generally enjoyed greater freedom than the first-time bride.

A man could choose his own wife when he was 18. But, unless his father was dead, in which case he was compelled to assume leadership of his family's household right away, he would usually wait until he was 30. It was then customary for the father to hand over the running of the household to his son. Until that time, a man lived in his father's house and was subject to his authority.

As at all key junctures in an ancient Greek's life, getting married was a protracted ritualistic affair. In Athens, a public pledge was made in the presence of witnesses in which the size and composition of the bride's dowry was laid down. Dowries were all-important, and it was a slight on a man's reputation if he proved unable to marry off his daughters or sisters because he could not afford a proper dowry. For poor people, help with dowries might come from wealthy relations or even friends. Dowries usually consisted of land or goods such as furniture.

Once the dowry was handed over, the couple were deemed to be irrevocably betrothed. Since Athenian girls were often engaged while they were still children, several years might elapse between the handing over of the dowry and the arrival of the girl in her groom's household. During this time the groom paid for his future wife's upkeep.

Another important stage in the process came when the bride was introduced to her fiancé's relations. On this occasion, an Athenian girl's pure Athenian blood was affirmed. The proceedings were solemnised by the groom making a sacrifice.

Tradition dictated a full moon and a winter month as the most auspicious times for nuptial festivities. The marriage ceremony began with a sacrifice at the bride's family home, during which the girl

WOMEN'S BUSINESS The virgin goddess Artemis presided over all the physical aspects of female life, including birth and death. Here she appears on the Parthenon frieze, around 440 BC.

PROTECTIVE INSTINCTS
A man dressed for travel leads his wife out on a rare excursion from her home.

consecrated her girdle to the virgin goddess Artemis to mark the end of her virgin's existence. Either at this point or earlier, on attaining marriageable age, girls also dedicated their toys to a goddess. Records survive of a girl called Timareta, who when she was about to be married consecrated her tambourines 'to thee, O Artemis of the Marshes . . . and the ball she was so fond of and her hairnet: her dolls, too, she has dedicated in a befitting manner, with her clothes – a virgin's offering to thee, O Virgin Goddess'. The principal rite in marriage was the bridal bath which also took place in the bride's home – a purification ceremony. A procession of women bearing torches went in front of a woman carrying a receptacle full of water from a sacred spring. While this was going on, the groom, too, was taking a ritual bath at his own family home.

The wedding feast that followed took place, without the groom, in the bride's home. The bride, who was veiled, wreathed and dressed in her best clothes, sat apart from the men with the other women – including one who had the special responsibility of guiding her through the proceedings. During the wedding feast, at which sesame cakes were served as a guarantee of fertility, a young boy whose parents were both alive, circled the guests dispensing bread and intoning: 'I have eschewed the worse; I have found the better.' The bride was congratulated by the assembled company,

A SHOCKING EXAMPLE OF LOVE

MANY ATHENIANS of the 5th century BC found the relationship between the statesman Pericles and his consort Aspasia deeply shocking. This was not so much because Aspasia had started her career as a courtesan and ended as a madam, nor because Pericles had divorced his first wife for her. Much more bizarre for the Athenians was the unconventional warmth and respect with which Pericles treated his new partner. As Plutarch noted: 'The story goes that he would kiss her warmly both when he left for the marketplace and when he returned home each day.' Rather than confining her to the women's quarters, Pericles lived with Aspasia and, most eccentrically of all, included her and the wives of his friends at his dinner parties. According to Plutarch, she was very good company, clever and politically astute: 'After all, Socrates sometimes visited her.'

Aspasia was an example of a courtesan who made good in a society where prostitution had thrived from the earliest times. Large Greek cities, particularly those on the coast with itinerant populations of sailors, played host to enormous numbers of prostitutes. The majority were slaves but some bought their freedom by borrowing money from past clients, and repaying the loan from their earnings; others were non-citizens but free women. Solon set up state brothels in Athens, run by registered slaves with prostitutes graded according to their earning potential. At the top of the hierarchy were the *hetairai* or 'companions', whose educated minds, artistic skills and physical beauty made their company preferable to that of legitimate wives – some even got invited to the normally all-male dinner parties. Aspasia was the most famous of these.

Top-grade courtesans could earn a lot of money: one was reputed to have commissioned a gold statue at Delphi which stood among those donated by generals and kings. But most prostitutes imported into male dining rooms could only command 1 obol, the smallest unit of currency, for their services. For these women, old age was a fearsome prospect: some bought female slaves or adopted abandoned baby girls whom they trained to support them when their bloom had faded. One was said to be 'highly skilled in picking out future beauties on the strength of their appearance in infancy'. But generally, the absence of male protectors or effective contraception made the prostitute's career dangerous.

NEW GUARDIAN   A cosmetic box shows a bridal procession as a groom escorts his bride from her father's home.

and at nightfall the groom arrived to carry her off in a nuptial cart, sandwiched between himself and his best man. A torchlit procession accompanied them singing hymns in honour of Hymen, the god of marriage.

On arrival at the groom's house, the couple were showered with nuts and dried figs and the bride was offered a cake of sesame and honey – both of them symbols of fertility. The climax of the proceedings came when the bride took off her veil. Then the groom led her into a wedding chamber guarded by a friend – to ensure that no one interrupted the consummation. The following day, the bride's parents arrived in procession to deliver their daughter's wedding presents.

Spartan marriages were much more brutal. In the words of the historian Plutarch: 'Women get married by being abducted, not when they are small and under-age but when they are in their prime and ripe. When the bride has been abducted the bridesmaid, as she is called, takes hold of her and shaves her hair off . . . dresses her in a man's cloak and sandals and puts her to be on a pallet alone and in the dark. Then the bridegroom slips quietly into the room . . . unloosens her girdle, and, raising her up, carries her over to the bed. After

DRESSING UP   A girl prepares for her wedding, having eaten a many-seeded fruit to ensure fertility.

spending a short amount of time with her, he departs discreetly to wherever he was previously accustomed to spend the night in order to bed down with the rest of his comrades.'

LIVING TOGETHER

Most ancient Greeks assumed that the key to a happy marriage was the wife's submission to her husband. Ideally 'authority, mastery and domination' were allied to female 'like-mindedness or compatibility' in a relationship which Plutarch compared to that of a horse and his rider.

Since men spent most of their days away from home, conjugal contact was limited. Plutarch advocated sexual intercourse between a man and his wife three times a month. But men were often away at war and even when they were not, once they had a family they could support, they were likely to sleep separately from their wives. In Athens, male infidelity was accepted so long as it was confined to non-citizen women. As the orator Demosthenes

KEEPING IT IN THE FAMILY

An heiress – a girl with no brothers to inherit her father's property – married her next of kin, even if he was an uncle. This custom, which made sure the property stayed in the family, often generated ruthless competition: at least two men are known to have divorced existing wives to marry an heiress. But it worked both ways. The next of kin was also obliged to marry a poor heiress – inheriting only her father's debts – unless he could supply the wherewithal to attract another husband.

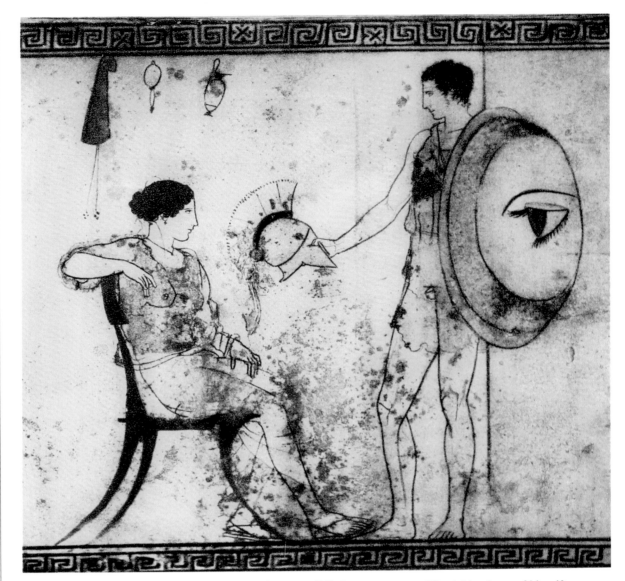

OFF TO THE WARS An Athenian vase from the 5th century BC shows a young soldier taking leave of his wife.

noted: 'We have prostitutes for physical excitement, mistresses to look after our daily comforts and wives to procreate legitimate children and to act as trustworthy custodians for our households.'

Despite the ordeal of their marriages, Spartan women generally enjoyed greater freedom than Athenians. They married men nearer their own age, and, since the husband went on living with his army group until he was 30, they were thoroughly experienced at household management by the time he finally arrived at the home. More significantly, they were allowed to own property and by the 4th century BC had amassed two-fifths of the land in Sparta.

In Athens, a husband could divorce his wife, if she failed to produce an heir, simply by throwing her out of the house. In theory, a woman, too, could end her marriage, by leaving her husband's home. But in practice, she needed the support of her father, to whom she would return, and the sanction of an archon (magistrate).

HAVING CHILDREN
The Greeks took a fairly clinical view of marriage and childbearing. 'Surely you do not suppose that it is for sexual satisfaction that men and women breed children,' wrote Xenophon, 'since the streets are full of people who will satisfy that appetite, as are the brothels? No, it is clear that we enquire into which women we may beget the best children from, and we come together with them and breed children.'

enduring labour with fortitude should struggle effectively and easily with labour pangs'.

Throughout her confinement, the pregnant woman gave special attention to the many gods who patronised reproduction. These could be sought in streams or rivers, giving wives a rare opportunity to venture outside the home, and included both Olympian and earth deities.

The birth took place at home in the women's quarters with female relations, friends and neighbours gathered together to give moral and physical support. Men were banned throughout. The midwife controlled the event with a mixture of ritual, superstition and incantations. Historians have calculated that between 10 and 20 per cent of mothers died giving birth. In Sparta, women who died in childbirth were honoured on gravestones in the same way as soldiers who died at war; both had given their lives in seeking to perpetuate the state.

An Athenian baby who survived the ordeal was immediately swaddled from neck to toe in bands, to restrain it from making violent movements that might distort its limbs, topped by a little pointed cap. The baby remained in swaddling bands for 60 days after birth. The birth of a boy was announced to the outside world by hanging an olive crown – the prize for victory at the Olympic games – on the entrance. The arrival of a girl, on the other hand, was shown by a small piece of woollen material, symbolic of her

COTTAGE INDUSTRY Idle women were disapproved of. Even upper-class women spun and wove for the home.

Childbirth itself, however, was a dangerous business. Many girls gave birth while still in their teens, and this combined with a complete ignorance of the connection between dirt and ill-health meant that frequently both mother and child died. Conception, pregnancy and labour therefore inspired a disproportionate amount of medical literature as well as many superstitious practices.

Weather conditions at the time of conception, the type of food consumed and the time of the year, month or day – all were cited by the medical fraternity as relevant to the health of the future baby. Sensibly enough, Aristotle recommended daily exercise and a healthy diet for pregnant women. In Sparta, according to Plutarch, the regime for expecting mothers included running, wrestling and jumping so that 'the root of what they have conceived [the foetus] should have a strong beginning in strong bodies and that they themselves by

THE ROLE OF THE MIDWIFE

MIDWIFERY WAS one of the few professions open to women. Despite the extensive powers of the midwife, or 'cord-cutter', being too old to bear more children of her own was the only qualification she needed. According to Socrates (whose mother had been a midwife), this was because the childless goddess Artemis 'assigned the privilege to women who were past childbearing years out of respect to their likeness to herself'. It was also believed that regular exposure to the pollution associated with childbirth resulted in sterility and so older women would not be at risk.

On arrival in a home, the midwife set about purifying the home in general and the women's quarters in particular. She brought drugs and a knowledge of incantations with which she claimed to alleviate labour pains, control delivery time and, if appropriate, provoke a miscarriage in the case of a stillborn child. Once the child had been born, she looked it over and gave her expert opinion on whether or not it should be raised. Then she announced to the father the arrival of his child.

The midwife's position enabled her to act as a go-between for sterile women or those who had borne stillborn children and mothers with babies who did not wish to raise them. The playwright Aristophanes (c.450-c.385 BC) even claimed that some women feigned pregnancy and then smuggled in another's child without the unsuspecting husband being any the wiser.

PERILOUS UNDERTAKING A midwife cradles a successfully delivered baby.

future domestic duties. Announcing the birth in this way also warned outsiders of the pollution within. A woman was considered 'unclean' throughout her confinement.

As soon as possible after delivery, the new mother visited the gods or goddesses with whom she had been in contact throughout her pregnancy (religious business being one of the few reasons for which respectable women were allowed out of the home), as well as the nymph at the holy stream whose waters she had drunk as a fertility aid. One 3rd-century couple gave thanks thus: 'The son of Kichesias dedicated sandals to you, Artemis, and [his wife] Themistodike [dedicated] simple folded woollen garments, lady, because you came gently to her when she was in labour, without your bow, and held your two hands above her.' They politely express the hope that Artemis will see to it that the father 'should live to see his baby boy wax strong in limb as a young man'.

EXPOSED TO THE ELEMENTS

For the ancient Greeks, the newborn baby was not yet a person, and therefore had no unquestionable right to live until it had been ceremonially integrated into the household five days after its birth. First of all, though, the father had to decide whether to raise the child or not. If he decided that the child was not wanted, the solution was extreme and,

HAPPY EVENT The men of a household arrive in the women's quarters to admire a new baby. Only Spartan babies were unswaddled.

to modern feelings, barbaric: the baby was left to die of exposure on, say, a hillside. In Sparta, according to Plutarch: 'Offspring were not reared at the will of the father, but were taken and carried by him to a place called Lesche, where the elders of the tribes officially examined the infant, and if it was well-built and sturdy, they ordered the father to rear it, and assigned it one of the [state's] 9000 plots of land; but if it was ill-born and deformed, they sent it to the so-called Apothetae, a chasm-like place at the foot of Mount Taygetus, in the conviction that the life of that which nature had not well equipped at the very beginning for health and strength was of no advantage to itself or the state.'

Girl babies were more at risk than their brothers because the need to furnish them with dowries made them a drain on family resources. One Greek soldier from the 1st century BC was unequivocal in the letter he wrote to his pregnant wife: 'If you happen to give birth, if it is a boy let it be, but if it is a girl cast it out.' Nevertheless, Greek laws – which ruled that the family's inheritance should be divided equally among sons – may have prompted some families to rid themselves of surplus boys, rather than see the family land frittered away into untenable lots. Sickly or deformed babies – the latter were thought to be the punishment of the gods, particularly for oath breaking – were at risk, too.

Despite their pragmatism, the Greeks did view the task of exposure as repellent, as is seen in many myths where people delegated to expose children find themselves unable to do so. Wherever possible, a slave or the midwife was charged with the task. The infant would be taken outside the city, town or village in a clay pot and either left exposed to the elements and wild beasts or placed at a crossroads or outside a shrine in the hope that a priest or passer-by would take pity on the baby and rear it. Many childless couples may well have been delighted to discover a healthy baby through whom they could continue their family line; others picked up discarded babies to raise as slaves, while priests sometimes adopted them to train as assistants. By the late 5th and early 4th centuries BC, the ethics of exposure were being questioned. Both Sophocles and Euripides made it known that they abhorred the practice.

GIVING THANKS After confinement a mother visited the river nymph whose protection she had solicited throughout her pregnancy.

CEREMONIES AFTER BIRTH

Five days after birth, the infant was formally admitted into the household at the *Amphidromia* ceremony, when the parents ran around the household hearth bearing the child in their arms. The religious significance of this lay in the fact that fire was the purifier, the hearth was at the centre of the home, and the goddess of the hearth, Hestia, protected both the family and their dwelling. It was a festive occasion, with friends and relations carousing and bestowing lucky charms that were tied around the baby's neck to ward off ill-health, misfortune and the evil eye.

On the tenth day, the baby was given its name. The Greeks only used one name, with most boys being given that of their paternal grandfathers. From now on, the child would be known as X son of Y of the locality Z, as in Pericles son of Xanthippus of Cholargus. Because the stock of names was limited, they were often duplicated – hence the need to distinguish them by their fathers' names.

WEANING Leather or cloth teats were attached to feeding bottles from which thirsty babies sometimes drank heavily diluted wine.

GROWING UP AND SCHOOLING

A son's education and a daughter's chastity were of prime importance to fathers.

While boys went to school to equip them for future citizenship,

girls stayed at home to learn the domestic skills they would need as wives and mothers.

THE FIRST YEARS of life were a very risky time in ancient Greece, and a sad time for many parents. Most couples could expect to lose at least one child in infancy, often carried away shortly after birth by a diarrhoea-related disease caused by dirty water and inadequate sewage disposal. Careful parents took measures such as commending their children to the patronage of a river god – running water being associated with fertility and growth. Later they would give the god thanks if their children had made it safely into adulthood.

At the same time, although child mortality was high, there were proportionately more children in Greek communities than in modern ones, since war casualties were constantly cutting into the adult male population – the average age among free male citizens was no more than 25. This left many fatherless children, called orphans even if their mothers were still living. In Athens, such orphans were supported by the state at the comparatively meagre rate of 1 obol a day if their fathers had been killed in war (the lowliest of unskilled workers was paid 3 obols a day); in other cases, it was the duty of relations to ensure that the child was at least not destitute.

As in many ancient cultures, sons were more valued than daughters because they continued the family line. They were also vital for fulfilling the military and political demands of the state. As a result, a fall in the birthrate after about 500 BC was a cause of great concern. In Sparta, a fighting force estimated at 8000 in the 5th century BC had been reduced to less than 1000 by 371 BC. In the case of Sparta, historians attribute this depopulation partly to the concentration of land in the hands of the few, leaving an impoverished majority unwilling to sire extra mouths to feed.

TENDER LOVE FOR A PET A young girl cherishes two doves in this memorial stone. Other popular pets included dogs, geese, hares and monkeys.

28

MOTHER LOVE A nurse (above) hurries to deliver a child into its mother's outstretched arms, on a vase from the mid-5th century BC. The ancient Greeks usually pictured children (left) as miniature adults with disproportionately small heads.

In any event, the general childlessness appeared to threaten the very existence of states and demanded extraordinary measures to encourage parents to fill the gap. The Spartan authorities even went so far as to encourage wife-sharing, particularly in the case of infertile marriages between old men and young girls. The older husband would be pressured into bringing in a younger man to impregnate his wife.

SLAVES AND NURSES

The children of rich parents spent much of their time in the company of slaves in the female quarters. They were suckled and looked after by wet nurses who were often much-loved members of the household valued by mother and children alike.

HARD TIMES FOR BACHELORS

Staying a bachelor was not illegal in Sparta, but it was not encouraged. Men who remained unmarried were banned from the treat of watching young people parade at a festival called the Gymnopaidia. In winter, they were forced to strip and march about denouncing themselves. If they reached old age, they were not shown the respect the Spartans usually accorded to the aged.

During her husband's daily absence from the home or while he was away at war, a rich woman might well become dependent on the nurse for company. Nurses were also expected to have such powers as the magic skills needed to protect a child from the evil eye. They could be slaves or free professionals. Frequently they were maintained until their death in their owner's or employer's home, as in one surviving tombstone inscription that states: 'Mikkos provided for . . . his good wet nurse as long as she lived and even in her old age. When she died he set up a dedication for future generations to see. So the old woman departs from this life, having received due recompense for her breasts.' Spartan nurses were considered particularly good at their job and could command top salaries in Athens.

In addition to milk from their wet nurses, babies might be given a porridge of flour and water mixed with wine and sweetened with honey. This was further diluted with milk – human, rather than animal, since it was believed that character was passed through milk. This mixture was fed to the babies from cumbersome feeding bottles resembling Aladdin lamps made of black glazed-ware. One such bottle is inscribed with the Greek word for 'Mummy', followed by the order: 'Drink, don't drop it.'

TIME FOR PLAY Toys were made at home and buried with the child if he or she died young. They might include rattles (such as the terracotta pig above) and various dolls. An Athenian marble relief (left) shows a boy playing with a wooden hoop.

Babies slept in wicker baskets or in a kind of wooden trough, and were rocked to sleep or soothed with lullabies. They might sit in terracotta high chairs – one example is fitted with a potty underneath.

Girls were generally less indulged than boys, as the Athenian writer Xenophon observed: 'Most Greeks expect *korai* [young girls] to keep their mouths shut and attend to their wool in the manner of the majority of skilled workers.'

Rocking horses, hoops, miniature carts, spinning tops, rattles, models of horses on wheels, and boats or dolls with jointed limbs were all typical presents from a parent to a child. Favourite games included knucklebones played with the ankle joints of cloven-footed animals. The five small, prettily shaped bones were thrown into the air, one at a time, and had to be caught on the back of the hand. People also played blindman's buff and a game called 'cooking pot'. A child sat on a pot while his friends circled and ridiculed him, until he managed to touch one of them with his foot.

Another game was a variation of piggyback. You started by throwing stones at a target. The child whose shot landed farthest from the mark was blindfolded and had to find his way to the target with another child on his back. There was also the equivalent of heads-and-tails in which a pot, glazed on one side, was used instead of a coin. Ball games were played with inflated pigs' bladders and one picture shows children playing a game that looks rather like cricket. Birds, dogs, geese, cocks, hares, goats and monkeys were among the Greeks' favourite pets.

STERN DISCIPLINE

Since children were regarded as lacking both intelligence and common sense, stern discipline was believed to prevent them from becoming wilful and self-indulgent. Accordingly, beating was regarded as perfectly acceptable. Mothers also conjured up monstrous figures with which to subdue their offspring. In one play an Alexandrian housewife invokes a creature called Mormo, who has big ears and a changing face and who walks like an animal, to control her difficult child.

Fathers had almost absolute powers over their children. By law, an Athenian child was completely subject to his or her father, and until the beginning of the 6th century BC, a father could sell his children into slavery. Even after that date, a daughter could be sold if she was discovered to be involved in an illicit sexual relationship.

In practice, however, a society in which the father was frequently absent left much responsibility for child-rearing in the hands of the mother. As one Spartan widow complained of her late husband: 'Indeed we had children but he never saw them other than as a farmer sees an outlying field at seed-time and when harvesting.' Spartan mothers had a reputation for exerting extreme moral pressure on their sons. The most famous instance is the mother who, on giving her son his shield to take into battle, grimly instructed him to return 'either with this or on this' – a coward would throw away his shield to run away faster, while dead warriors were borne home lying on their shields.

COMING OF AGE

Adolescence was as difficult a time for Greek youngsters as it is for any modern teenager. With puberty, it was thought, boys and girls became susceptible for the first time to adult diseases from which they had previously been immune. And, like their modern counterparts, Greek parents discovered that their offspring were emotionally volatile at this age. Plutarch records 'a sudden yearning for death, a manic desire to hang themselves' which broke out among young girls in the city of Miletus

FEMININE PURSUITS Household duties started young for most Greek girls, but this young woman takes a rare moment of leisure to play a juggling ball game.

YOUNG ANGLER A boy, equipped with rod, creel and lobster pot feels a bite on his line on a pot from the 5th century BC.

– on the Aegean coast of modern Turkey. Nobody knew how to staunch this epidemic which was attributed to some freak quality of the air, until it was suggested that the naked bodies of the dead girls should be paraded through the streets: a prospect so shameful to those who were still alive that the suicide attempts came to an immediate end.

Generally, Greek girls achieved a safe haven from such perils within marriage, which usually happened when they were about 15 years old. Before that, however, there were some exclusively female rites of passage performed by pubescent girls. One of the most extraordinary of these ceremonies was that known as the *Arkteia* ('She-Bear Ceremony') in which young Athenian girls dressed in saffron robes to imitate the tawny hide of a she-bear and performed ritual acts in honour of the goddess Artemis. The story that gave rise to this ceremony told of a she-bear that was tamed and lived in the sanctuary of Artemis. Unfortunately, the bear tore out the eye of a young girl, whose brothers proceeded to kill it in revenge. This angered Artemis and in her anger she sent a plague to afflict the people of Athens. When the citizens went to an oracle to find a remedy for their predicament, it suggested that Athenian fathers should make their daughters act in a bear-like manner as a sign of atonement.

On the island of Chios, marriageable young girls were obliged to dance and disport themselves in special sanctuaries while being sized up by potential suitors; at night they took turns to travel from house to house in order to wait upon each others' parents and brothers 'even to the extent of washing their feet', according to the historian Plutarch. In some places, girl choirs gave teenage girls a brief social life, later curtailed in marriage. The most famous of these circles was dominated by the female

FESTIVE PROCESSION A frieze from the Parthenon shows a group of women during the annual Panathenaean Festival.

poet Sappho on the island of Lesbos. In the 6th century BC, she gathered around her a group of girls to dance and sing and composed love poetry for them.

For boys, meanwhile, education was dominated by the poet Homer. The Greeks believed that Homer's two epic poems, the *Iliad*, describing the Trojan war of about 1100 BC, and the *Odyssey*, telling of the wily hero Odysseus' adventure-prone return from Troy, were true histories. In describing the actions of his heroes, Homer had set out a system of values that was imported wholesale into the education of the Greece of the 5th century BC. The curriculum was essentially Homeric, with an early emphasis on physical prowess, music and reciting passages from the great poet. Later, public speaking was added to the various skills taught in cities such as Athens, as the change from an aristocratic to a democratic society demanded the ability to influence the mass of people.

Above all, the Homeric code of ethics taught the love of glory and the need to win at all costs – even if life itself, to which the Greeks were so passionately attached, had to be sacrificed along the way.

This desire for glory defined the Greek hero. The two principal characters in the *Iliad*, Achilles and Hector, both know from childhood prophecies that they are fated to die early and both bewail that destiny. But when the time comes for them to lay down their lives, they do so unhesitatingly, not out of patriotic duty, but because not to do so would dishonour them.

This competitive spirit permeated most aspects of life in the 5th century, from sport to intellectual feats such as composing poetry or plays. In the case of the Spartans, however, things were slightly different, for while their state was second to none in its emphasis on military prowess, it had less concern by that time with the arts. Indeed, 5th-century Spartans even went

GAMES OF YOUTH
A statue from the late 4th century BC shows two adolescent girls playing piggyback.

HEROES AND MENTORS

IN ARISTOCRATIC CIRCLES, an older youth would help to guide a boy through the transition from childhood to adulthood. This tradition was an ancient one, elevated and sacred, that had evolved from the warrior-comradeship of the Homeric heroes – an example is the loving relationship between Achilles and his friend Patrocolus. It continued in modified form until the 4th century BC and after.

In a society that did little to teach its boys ethical values at home, such liaisons had a vital educational role. Public opinion held the older youth responsible for the moral development of the younger boy; in Sparta he was punishable by law if his protégé failed to behave as was thought proper. Plutarch records two instances in which older youths were penalised when their cowardly protégés respectively screamed in pain at the gymnasium and in battle.

The ideal that lay behind the relationships was well expressed by Socrates' pupil Xenophon: 'By the very fact that we breathe our love into beautiful boys, we keep them away from avarice, increase their enjoyment in work, trouble and dangers, and strengthen their modesty and self-control.'

A male relationship usually ended when the older man married, but while it lasted, the relationship was all-important. In Sparta, a boy who failed to attract an older friend was supposed to be morally deficient, while an older youth who did not adopt a younger boy was no less severely condemned.

It was considered demeaning for the younger man to accept presents from an admirer, and both parties refrained from excessive or impulsive tokens of affection. So an older man who made a nuisance of himself by serenading the object of his admiration at the latter's home was to be despised.

It was, however, acceptable for a lover to inscribe the name of his beloved on bathhouse walls, trees or the rim of a fine plate. Sometimes, the inscriptions were crude – the Greeks habitually called a spade a spade – but some beautiful grave inscriptions testify to the loftiness of the affection that could exist. One was written in the 1st century BC by the poet Crinagoras to a boy he named Eros after Aphrodite's son, the god of love: 'For Eros himself gave both his name and his beauty to the boy who lies here beneath a heap of clods. O earth, crowded with tombs, do thou lie light on the boy and do thou lie hushed for his sake.'

The alliances were not always consummated, sometimes confining themselves to kissing, noble sentiments and languishing looks. The Greeks responded to beauty with an extraordinary intensity, and both boys and girls were regarded as reaching the peak of physical perfection in their adolescence. Every year threw up a number of outstandingly handsome boys and everyone in the city knew their names. The youthful loveliness of the Athenian politician Alcibiades acquired almost mythological fame.

BODY BEAUTIFUL A plate from the 6th century BC shows a victorious young athlete being congratulated by his trainer.

At their best, these were ennobling relationships. As Plato put it: 'I cannot say what greater benefit can fall to the lot of a young man than a virtuous lover and to the lover than a beloved youth.' He also wrote: 'If then there were any means whereby a state or army could be formed of lovers and favourites, they would administer affairs better than all others . . . And such men together with others like them, though few in number, so to speak would conquer the world.' This ideal was not all airy nonsense. The Theban army known as the 'Sacred Band' was made up of 300 well-born men who had sworn love for each other. They were famously brave soldiers who fought together for 35 years inspiring the respect of Alexander the Great.

SPARE THE ROD . . . A vase from the late 6th century BC shows a man beating a boy with a sandal. The ancient Greeks believed in firm discipline.

so far as to pride themselves on their illiteracy as a sign of their militaristic dedication.

Spartan education was above all designed to produce a faultless killing machine, manned by soldiers who, according to Plutarch, were 'obedient to the word of command, capable of enduring hardship and victorious in battle'. They did indeed become the best fighting force in Greece. One means of achieving this was a tough domestic regime. Until he was seven, the Spartan boy remained at home, where he had to eat what was on his plate, not cry or show any other form of emotion, be fearless of the dark and not care about being left alone. Then at the age of seven, he was torn away from his home and sent to live in communal barracks with other boys, where he remained, without holidays, until he was 30.

As soon as he arrived at school, the Spartan boy was enrolled in a series of military-style organisations that kept him active throughout his childhood and adolescence. From 8 to 11 he was a 'little boy', accountable to the senior boys who took on a punishing parental role; from his 12th to his 15th-birthday he was an 'adolescent'; and from 16 to 20 an *eiren* – a rank divided into first, second, third, fourth and fifth-year grades.

LIFE IN THE BEEHIVE

According to Plutarch, Spartan citizens were trained so 'that they had no wish to live alone and lost even the capacity for doing so; like bees they were always united behind their leaders for the public good'. Children always had someone in authority over them and were automatically deferential to any adult they encountered. In such a regime, a boy needed only the most rudimentary literary skills or, as Plutarch put it, 'enough to get by with'. Any form of individualism was discouraged. The contrast between Sparta and Athens in educational styles was

IN THE GOOD OLD DAYS

FOR ATHENIAN conservatives, an old-fashioned education was the best preparation a young boy could have for the responsibilites of adult life. A crusty character from Aristophanes' play *The Clouds* recalls the decorum of a traditional schooling:

❝ I'll tell you about the way boys were brought up in the old days . . . First of all, children were supposed to be seen and not heard. Then, all the boys of the district were expected to walk together through the streets to their music-master's, quietly and decorously, and without a coat, even when it was snowing confetti – and they did. And when they got there he made them learn some of the old songs by heart . . . singing them to the traditional tunes their father used . . . And if any of them did anything disreputable such as putting in chromatic bits, all tied up in knots . . . why, he was given six of the best for insulting the Muses. . . . They weren't allowed to grab the best vegetables at dinner either, like the dill and parsley – those were always reserved for their elders and betters. In fact they ate no fancy stuff at all. ❞

summarised by an anonymous writer in the 5th century BC: 'The Lacedaemonians [Spartans] consider it a bad thing for children to learn music and reading and writing, whereas the Ionians [Athenians] think it is shocking if they do not know these things.' Instead, the Spartan emphasis was on physical strength. Starting with gymnastics, the boy rapidly moved on to military drills, learning how to move in formation, to carry weapons, to wield the spear and other muscle-building skills. He was also encouraged to fight with other boys.

When they were 11, Spartan boys' already austere regime grew even harsher. Their skins became hardened from the scanty protection given by their clothes – they were not allowed to wear a tunic and were given only one cloak a year. Shaven-headed and marching barefoot, the boys were savagely whipped by their minders for the smallest offence. Whatever the season, they stripped naked for games, and were only allowed to bathe or anoint their bodies with oil on infrequent festival days. They were deliberately fed inadequate portions of revolting food, thereby encouraging them to supplement their diet by stealth. There is a story of a child who was caught with a stolen fox under his shirt. Rather than admit to his crime, he allowed

the animal to chew through his stomach – with fatal results.

The most savage custom of all for Spartan boys was that of the *krypteia,* or 'period of concealment'. Boys spent time hiding out in the countryside by themselves, where they stalked helots, members of the Spartan slave-race, like wild animals. The object was to kill at least one of them.

Spartan girls, meanwhile, had their own toughening ordeals to go through – though these resulted in a much more egalitarian education than that of their counterparts in Athens. As with boys, the emphasis was on physical fitness rather than artistic skills. Spartan girls wrestled and threw the discus and javelin, so that they would develop into strapping women who could produce future soldiers for the state. They were

VALOROUS PURSUITS   A bowl of the 6th century
BC shows a Homeric hero battling valorously
against a monstrous snake.

discouraged from harbouring any feminine sensibilities by parading near-naked in front of the men and by taking a prominent part in the dancing and singing at religious festivals.

AT SCHOOL IN ATHENS

In Homer's Greece of the 8th century BC, equestrian skills and music had formed the basic curriculum of the very rich. And even after literacy had grown in importance, many aristocratic families in Athens and many other Greek states continued to yearn for the old privileged traditions. In Aristophanes' play *The Clouds* (423 BC) a mother eagerly anticipates her son racing through the streets in the old-fashioned way in his chariot with his long robe flying. Her husband, however, is more up-to-date in his outlook and is appalled that her influence has turned his son into a horse-mad fop: 'He has long hair, drives a two-horse chariot and dreams about horses when he's asleep.'

In much the same way, the aristocratic poet Pindar (513-438 BC), who composed triumphal odes in honour of sporting champions, mirrored the opinion of a large reactionary group when he derided the idea of education not only for the noble class but also for all other citizens. Education for an aristocrat, he argued, enabled him to take up the leadership role expected of him. For the rest – 'those who know only because they have lessons' – there was no point in refinement because they had no innate nobility of spirit on which to build.

Despite the reservations of the conservatives, a number of privately run schools were available in some cities by the 5th century BC. Herodotus, for instance, mentions a school that had 120 pupils in 494 BC. Since teachers were lowly paid professionals, most people could afford the services of a man whose only qualification for his job was his literacy. School was generally held in the master's house, with hours of opening and numbers of pupils carefully stipulated by the state.

At all levels of the free citizen body, it was increasingly expected that every boy should at least learn to read and write in order to discharge his civic duties: even a sausage-maker, according to Aristophanes, could do so. Writing was needed by men – the seclusion of women meant that literacy was not a skill they needed – for activities that ranged from making shopping lists (since shopping was a male prerogative in ancient Greece) and composing poetry to inscribing tombstones and cursing enemies. The result was that most of Athens' male population was literate.

Children of both sexes spent their first six years or so within the women's quarters of the home where they were taught whatever their mothers or other female relations had to impart. This is where girls of all classes would stay for their entire childhood, acquiring the domestic skills they would need for their married lives. Boys, on the other hand, might go off to school when they were seven. If a boy came from a rich family, he would be accompanied by his pedagogue – usually an elderly slave – who was responsible for his good behaviour and always escorted him outside the home. The slave carried his satchel – containing wax writing tablets, a stylus and, when the boy grew older, a lyre. He stayed with his charge until the end of the school day.

There were no weekend breaks and holidays were restricted to the festival days that came thick and fast in some months but were much scarcer in

LEARNING HOW TO WRITE

Greek schoolboys wrote on wax tablets with an instrument called a stylus. This was pointed at one end for writing, and flattened at the other end so the pupil could erase mistakes. The tablets might be single or double-sided, and there might be several leaves hinged together. The master would sketch the letters faintly for the child to trace over. Papyrus and ink were also used. The ink was made from soot mixed with resin and diluted with water by the master or one of his assistants. Pens were made from split and trimmed reeds.

others; almost half the days in the Greek equivalent of February were holidays.

There were three main areas of education: basic literacy with some arithmetic, music and physical education. Some schools offered training in all three, but parents might choose individual tutors for the different subjects. The teachers sat on throne-like seats and their pupils on three-legged stools, writing on their knees since there were no tables.

YOUTHFUL AMAZONS Spartan girls, unlike their Athenian counterparts, were never sheltered from the rigours of outdoor life. They developed into famously awesome women, having undergone tough physical training which included instruction in wrestling (above) and long-distance running (right).

HOW TO TEACH THE YOUNG

ETWEEN 390 and 380 BC, the philosopher Plato and orator Isocrates put forward two views of education. Their systems were very different – indeed, they stood in opposition to one another – yet both have had an immense influence on educational theory right up to the present day.

Plato, inspired by his own thwarted political ambitions, determined to provide Athens with future generations of great statesmen. To this end, he built an Academy around a sacred wood on the outskirts of the city. It consisted of a sprawling network of buildings, sports fields and colonnaded walks, in which a brotherhood of scholars imbibed the teachings of their beloved master. Plato is known to have favoured his pupils' active participation in lessons, rather than the passive indoctrination supported by old-style educationalists. Although students paid, Plato (a nobleman) did not run his school as a commercial enterprise. He covered his costs but, unlike the famous travelling teachers of his day, the Sophists, he never sought a profit.

Plato challenged the view that Homer was virtually all-knowing and that a knowledge of his works was the only education a man needed. This made him unpopular with his more traditionalist contemporaries. Combined with the leisure students needed to have at their disposal to attend the Academy and the intellectual demands made on them there, it meant that only a few people were familiar with Plato's ideas. His fame and influence mostly came after his death.

LOWLY PAID PROFESSION A bowl shows a schoolmaster equipped with a writing tablet and pen.

Plato also supported the idea of a state-run education system in which, from the kindergarten, girls and boys would be given an equal – though separately taught – training. In his ideal scheme of things students would receive the usual musical and gymnastic education until the age of 20. The brightest would then be selected to study mathematics for a further ten years. After that, the select band would be tested again to establish whether or not they were capable of embarking on the elitist world of dialectics (a special form of philosophical reasoning). After five years of initiation, Plato demanded that they should spend 15 years participating in civic life, always keeping a careful check on their moral health. Only then, at the age of 50, would they be ready to tackle the nature of pure goodness. As Plato observed: 'It was a long way round.'

Isocrates had greater influence among his contemporaries than Plato, making huge sums of money in the process. He would teach only five or six pupils at a time, thereby fostering an intimate atmosphere in his school. His pupils' devotion to him was so great that they found it difficult to leave him at the end of the course – or so Isocrates boasted. It is certainly true that the great strategist Timotheus erected a statue of his master at Eleusis 'in honour not only of his great intelligence but also the charm of his friendship'. Several other politicians, writers and orators emerged from Isocrates' school, with the result that by the end of his career he had educated a whole new political group.

Isocrates saw education as embracing both the body and intellect, as opposed to Plato who confined physical training to the elementary level. In this, Isocrates was more in tune with the thinking of ordinary people of his time. He also differed from Plato in advocating debating practice from an early age, rather than reserving it for an intellectual elite. His teaching was practical and realistic, aimed at equipping men for politics in their cities. Both men, however, stressed that an individual must have the basic mental ability for profitable study, whereas the travelling Sophists claimed to be able to work their magic on anyone, whatever their intelligence.

Isocrates also differed from many Sophists in his concern with the moral content of speeches. In his hands, the art of oratory evolved into ethics. 'The right word,' he argued 'is a sure sign of good thinking.' He was convinced, too, that education contributed to the development of character and moral fibre.

HEADS DOWN Two boys learn music and writing from their teachers. A pedagogue (far right) is in attendance.

Learning by rote was the teacher's chief technique. The children were made to recite the letters of the Greek alphabet – *alpha, beta, gamma, delta,* and so on – that had been adopted from the Phoenicians in the 8th century BC. This they did over and over again, fixing them in their minds with a series of memory-aiding rhymes.

The letters were particularly important because they were used not only to denote words but also figures and even musical intervals. Slowly the boy would progress from single letters to two, three and four-letter syllables, using spelling books in which each word was broken up to facilitate pronunciation. Reading was made harder by texts – papyrus rolls rather than books – that had no punctuation at all and the words were not divided by spaces. A child always read out aloud even to himself and would continue to do so as an adult, unless he could get a slave to do the job for him.

Arithmetic existed only in a rudimentary form because the Greeks had never grasped the notion of zero. Nevertheless, with the aid of the abacus and their

ATHENA WRITING Unlike the goddess, most Greek women were illiterate.

fingers, boys could add, subtract, divide and multiply. They probably even knew some fractions – for example that the drachma was worth 6 obols and that a quarter-drachma was therefore worth 1½ obols – enough to do the shopping at any rate.

Music was a crucial part of the syllabus, as it had been for Homer's Greeks. It predated the teaching of literary skills and continued to have an almost hypnotic effect on the Greeks of the 5th century BC: vase-paintings show men apparently mesmerised by musicians. Music was the glorious wrapping for epic poetry: 'All men who dwell on earth owe a bard honour and respect,' the Homer's Odysseus reminds the people of Phaeacia where he has been wrecked, 'for the Muse has planted the gift of song in his heart, and cherishes all like him'. Most people could afford musical training for their offspring, and to play an instrument was the mark of a cultured man. Any musical innovation provoked anxious rumblings among those who saw it as the glue of their society.

The lyre was the favoured instrument of the educated classes who engaged special music masters to teach their children how to play it. Since beat took priority over the variety of notes, instruction was not as difficult as it sounds. The lyre was a stringed instrument, with a cavity originally formed from a tortoise shell. Seven strings were attached to struts and raised by a bridge. The player plucked the strings with his fingers or struck cords with a small stick tied to the instrument with ribbon, while singing the words from the old lyric poets in accompaniment.

As well as providing scope for competition, physical skills and fitness were vital for a race who spent so much time at war. When he was 12, the Athenian boy went to the *palaestra* – an open-air sportsground surrounded by walls. Here, the boys were initiated into gymnastics and sports training. They stripped in covered changing rooms, sponged themselves down at a fountain or stone trough, and then covered their bodies with a film of oil and sand. The oil was used like soap and would be scraped off the body afterwards; the sand made it easier for a boy to be gripped by his opponent in wrestling. Only after they had washed and anointed themselves did the boys present themselves to the gym-master, an awesome figure in a purple cloak, who occasionally prodded recalcitrant pupils with a forked stick.

Often, the exercises were performed under a burning sun; at other times, the unpredictable Greek winds blew up clouds of choking dust as the gym-master demonstrated a variety of wrestling holds and positions. These generated an entire vocabulary with which every male Athenian was familiar. Boys were paired off to wrestle by lot, having previously loosened the soil of the arena with a spade to soften any falls – loosening the soil was also deemed to be good exercise for them. They attempted to throw their adversaries during three-round contests.

The gym-master also presided over the long jump – which

BALL CONTROL The rudiments of a ball game are being demonstrated on this mid-4th-century BC gravestone.

the boys did carrying dumb-bells made of stone or lead, thought to increase their momentum and thus the distance jumped – as well as running and sometimes boxing. Boys prepared themselves for boxing by tying strips of leather around their fists to make the fist more rigid and a more effective weapon.

It was an exhausting time for them, and though the master was careful not to push them too far, they were inevitably covered in a lather of sweat, oil and dust by the time they had finished. They then retreated to the benches in the rest rooms to clean off the dirt and oil with bronze scrapers and to douse themselves down with water once more.

LEARNING SOPHISTICATION

In the latter half of the 5th century BC, a group of travelling lecturers known as Sophists revolutionised teaching by introducing higher education for young men. Previously even a statesman such as Pericles or an intellectual such as Socrates had received little more than an elementary education. Now, however, young men could embark on three- or four-year courses that in some cases promised to transform them into accomplished statesmen. This was particularly important in Athens where, under the guidance of Pericles, democracy put down deeper roots and politics became more of a passion for most citizens. Here, political success came to usurp the old heroic ideal of individual valour in battle as the means of fulfilling male ambition.

The Sophists converged on Athens, gathering around them pupils from the city and others they had collected during publicity tours around the country towns round about. Plato disparaged their utilitarian focus on 'the education of men', as opposed to his own abstract quests after truth, but

SPEEDING Boys took part in races over distances from 200 yd (180 m) to 3 miles (4.8 km).

even he could not deny the electrifying effect they had on Athenian youth. Anyone could enrol himself with the master of his choice, provided he could pay the fees. Protagoras (*c*.485-411 BC) – said to have coined the maxim 'Man is the measure of all things' – was the first to sell his skills in this way and commanded huge amounts for courses in good citizenship. According to Plato, he 'made more money than [the renowned sculptor] Pheidias with all his lovely works and ten other sculptors put together'.

The Sophists marketed themselves by travelling to different towns and famous sanctuaries such as Delphi that drew people from all over Greece. There they could be sure of finding ready-made audiences for their sample lectures. These either took the form of dazzling improvisations on a theme proposed by the crowd or carefully prepared speeches. Some like Hippias of Elis – who once claimed to have made everything he was wearing, including his ring and oil bottle – affected to be in possession of all knowledge. He certainly did know a lot about science, insisting that his pupils should study arithmetic, geometry, astronomy and acoustics – the four sciences that had been developed since the time of the pioneering philosopher and mathematician Pythagoras in the 6th century BC. Others, however, were unquestionably charlatans who used stage effects, such as an elevated throne or elaborate robes, to inspire awe among their potential clients.

The most influential part of the Sophists' teaching was the emphasis on rhetoric. The rhetoricians

ORIGINS OF SOPHISTICATION

The word 'sophisticated' derives from the name Sophist given to a number of philosophers and teachers who wandered ancient Greece instructing young people in ethics and the arts of public speaking. Their name derived, in turn, from the Greek word *sophos*, 'skilled, clever'. In fact, they were often accused of teaching over-clever and somewhat self-serving methods of argument – hence another English word, 'sophistry', for plausible but misleading reasoning.

instructed pupils in the tactical tricks of public speaking by giving them sample speeches to copy and study. The subject matter might range from singing the praises of cities or mice to standardised passages designed to flatter judges or dismiss evidence elicited under torture. But great prominence was also given to abstract themes, such as the nature of justice or injustice.

Because of their educational innovations, the Sophists aroused the profound distrust of the common people who perceived them as mercenary, sceptical and therefore a threat to the moral foundations of society. So, for example, Protagoras was treading on sensitive ground when he observed: 'As for the Gods, I do not know whether they exist or not. It is a difficult question and life is too short.' The playwright Aristophanes, who most nearly

FIGHTING CATS AND DOGS Some boys set a dog against a cat for a bout of cruel sport at the gymnasium. The relief comes from the base of an Athenian statue dating from around 510 BC.

HOLDING FORTH   A jar from the late 5th century BC shows a Sophist teacher mounted on a pedestal as he addresses his audience.

order to safeguard the individual from any mischance that might be sent by the gods. There were also a variety of checks and counterchecks to ensure that no outsiders could infiltrate themselves into the group of people with the right to citizenship in any particular state.

Most Greek cities divided their citizens into 'tribes'. Sparta had three. In about 507 BC, the lawgiver Cleisthenes had established ten in Athens, based on the area in which people lived rather than on blood relationships. Another set of groupings in Athens, which was based on blood relationship, consisted of the phratries, each of which was composed of a group of families. It was to his father's phratry that the Athenian boy was admitted as the first step of his formal integration into the adult world. For this, the entire group gathered together to witness him swearing to his pure and legitimate Athenian blood. With the inscription of his name on the phratry list, the boy found himself incorporated into an all-important social, political and religious circle to which he would henceforth turn whenever he was in trouble: if he was ever in need of witnesses, for instance, or of avengers for crimes against his property.

When they were 18, Athenian boys were enrolled with their *deme* (or village, another group based on where they lived) at an annual ceremony attended by all the other appropriately aged boys. This was the first time that a boy's existence was officially recognised (parents did not register their babies at birth) and he now attained the rights and responsibilities of citizen status.

Having reached the age of discretion and ceased to be subservient to the male head of his household, he was responsible for the first time before the law for any crime he might commit. This was a considerable step and not all potential demes-men achieved it, as Aristotle's *Constitution of Athens* makes clear: 'When they are being registered, their demes-men vote about the candidates on oath, first as to whether they appear to have reached the legal age – if they are regarded as not having done so they return to the *paides* [child status] – and

reflected the views of the ordinary citizen, denounced the Sophists as men who filled the hot-bath house and emptied the wrestling schools.

Nevertheless, the Sophists helped to mould a whole new generation of politicians in the late 5th century BC that was more highly trained and sceptical than any of its predecessors.

CEREMONIAL RITES OF PASSAGE

Between the ages of 16 and 18, Athenian boys were officially initiated into the adult world. As with all such turning points in the Greek's life, this transitional period was saturated with ceremonial in

THE DEATH OF SOCRATES

SOCRATES WAS condemned to death by Athenian political reactionaries on a trumped-up charge of worshipping gods different from those worshipped by the city and encouraging immoral attitudes among the young. In accordance with the custom of the time, he was given a death potion of hemlock to drink.

The philosopher Plato was ill at the time of Socrates' death and so not with him when it happened. But his harrowing description is based on the accounts of close friends who were there. It tells how, after having spent a day discussing Immortality with his friends, Socrates refuted his friends' suggestion that he should delay taking the poison:

❝ At this Crito [one of the friends] made a sign to his servant, who was standing near by. The servant went out and after spending a considerable time returned with the man who was to administer the poison; he was carrying it ready prepared in a cup. When Socrates saw him he said: "Well, my good fellow, you understand these things; what ought I to do?" "You have only to walk about until your legs are heavy, and then to lie down and the poison will act," said the jailor, at the same time handing the cup to Socrates. In the easiest and gentlest manner, without the least fear or change of colour or feature, he took the cup and said: "What do you say about making a libation out of this cup to any god? May I, or not?" The man answered: "We only prepare, Socrates, just so much as we deem

enough." "I understand," said he, "but I may and must ask the gods to prosper my journey from this to the other world – even so – and so be it according to my prayer." Then raising the cup to his lips he quite readily and cheerfully drank the poison. At this all his friends began to weep. Socrates alone retained his calmness. "What is this strange outcry?" he said. "I sent away the women mainly in order that they might not misbehave in this way, for I have been told that a man should die in peace. Be quiet, then and have patience." When we heard his words we were ashamed and refrained our tears; and he walked about until, as he said, his legs began to fail, and then he lay on his back according to the directions, and the man who gave him the poison, now and then looked at his feet and legs; and after a while he pressed his foot hard and asked him if he could feel; and [Socrates] said "No"; and then his leg and so upwards and upwards, and showed us that he was cold and stiff. And he felt them himself and said: "When the poison reaches the heart, that will be the end." He was beginning to grow cold about the groin, when

AN ADMIRABLE MAN Socrates lived and died in accordance with his principles.

he uncovered his face, for he had covered himself up, and said – they were his last words – he said: "Crito, I owe a cock to Asclepius; will you remember to pay the debt?"

"It shall be done", said Crito. "Are you sure that there is nothing else?"

Socrates made no reply to this question, but after a little while he stirred; and when the man uncovered him, his eyes were fixed. When Crito saw this, he closed the mouth and eyes.

Such, Echecrates, was the end of our comrade, who was, we may fairly say, of all those whom we knew in our time, the bravest and also the wisest and most upright man. ❞

secondly on whether the candidate is free and was born in accordance with the law.'

Another privilege was that boys could now recline as fully fledged guests at *symposia* – the all-male dining and drinking parties that were a favourite form of entertainment among wealthy Athenian men – rather than simply being brought on to serve the wine to their fathers' guests. In theory an 18-year-old could even marry without his father's consent, but since the father retained the right to to throw him out of the household and disinherit him it is unlikely that many youths exercised this prerogative.

There were other limits to the new-found freedoms of l8-year-old boys. They were still not thought to be mature enough to sit in the Assembly, for example, until after they had completed two years of military service. While they were doing their military service the *epheboi*, as the young soldiers were known, sported wide-brimmed hats and black travelling cloaks which denoted to everybody their new status as servants of the state. During their second year, they were given the important job of patrolling the state's frontier posts, scouting or repelling intruders.

After their service as epheboi, Athenians between the ages of 19 and 29 were called up to fight as hoplites (foot soldiers) more frequently than anyone else. Even so, they were still considered too immature for election to the governing Council or Boule. Outstandingly gifted young men like Alcibiades could and did make a name for themselves as political speakers while in their twenties, but they were mostly regarded with distrust that bordered

MOVING ON **Young girls process during a religious festival. These festivals provided one of the few opportunites for girls to leave the home.**

THE MORNING AFTER A boy cradles an older man's head as he vomits into a bucket after an alcoholic dinner.

on hatred. Generally speaking, rich young men wandered around in bands of their own age group, apportioning their time between the gymnasium, the wrestling school and the market-place during the day and men's dining rooms at night.

But for those whose fathers were killed at war, and many were, it was a different story. Such youths immediately became heads of their households. If they came from rich households, the responsibilities might be particularly onerous, especially for a boy who until then had barely been responsible even for himself. There might be outlying farms to manage and public duties to perform. One defendant in a court case claimed that on being admitted into his deme (village) he

was faced with a list of tasks that ranged from the production of a tragic drama and the funding of a group of dancers for a state festival to the organising and financing of three separate choirs for other festivals.

The position of their Spartan counterparts between the ages of 20 and 30 was much more restricted. They were not only ineligible for any kind of government office, but may also have been refused admission to the state Assembly. They continued to live under the rule of a group supervisor, although the supervisor could no longer punish them himself and had to refer disciplinary matters to the magistrates. They were allowed to grow their hair long but not to shop in the marketplace. Married men were still confined to a male dormitory and had to visit their wives in secret at night: 'Some begat children before they had seen their wives by daylight,' according to Plutarch.

From among men in the prime of their life, the chief magistrates (or ephors) chose three cavalry selectors who each appointed 100 young men to act as a regiment of 300. Their job was to be a bodyguard for the two hereditary kings who headed the Spartan state.

ELDERS AND THE ELDERLY

The family was responsible for the care of the elderly, although the state also

took care to legislate against their ill treatment. Old people were expected to live

active and productive lives – both at home and on behalf of the state – right up to the end.

SUDDENLY, at the age of 30, the Athenian male passed from youth to full maturity. The Greeks had no real conception of middle age. When Socrates once asked an acquaintance called Charikles to define how long young manhood lasted Charikles replied: 'Until [men] have reached the age when they are permitted to serve on the Council' – at their 30th birthday. Similarly, Spartans of this age were for the first time eligible for election as an ephor, one of the state's five chief magistrates. It was also at about 30 that Athenians traditionally got married.

CUT DOWN IN HIS PRIME An heroic early death, as illustrated on this late 5th-century BC bowl, was regarded as particularly glorious.

Old age began equally abruptly at 63 and, unlike youth, it was not a time of life that the Greeks gave much thought to. Doctors, for example, paid little attention to the illnesses to which old people were subject, although they did note some of the symptoms of old age. 'Difficulty in breathing, catarrh accompanied by coughing . . . arthritis . . . dizzy spells, apoplexy . . . itching of the whole body, sleeplessness, watery discharge from bowels, eyes and nostrils, dullness of vision . . . and hardness of hearing' are some of the manifestations referred to by the school of medicine founded by Hippocrates (c.460-c.370 BC) on the island of Cos.

Just as adolescents were believed to become susceptible suddenly to diseases from which they had previously been immune, so a 63-year-old, according to one handbook, was immediately in danger of developing gall stones, 'scrofulous swellings', haemorrhoids and other horrors.

For women, changes in lifestyle that came with advancing years were no less dramatic. A woman who had been through the menopause was for the first time allowed outside the female quarters unaccompanied. This was because she was past childbearing age and therefore no longer in need of such vigilant care to ensure her faithfulness to her husband.

Doctors were in general agreement that the female menopause occurred when the woman was in her forties. 'In the majority of women', observed one, 'menstruation ceases when they reach their 40th year but in those who exceed this age it can last up to their 50th and some women even give birth [at about this age].' Menopausal women were perceived as being mentally and physically unstable.

THE BURDEN OF AGE

The position of the elderly was an ambiguous one. With the Greek emphasis on beauty as well as a competitively productive life, those who were neither pleasing to look at nor capable of work were often viewed with revulsion. The poets, whose special subject was love and aesthetic pleasures, found them particularly difficult to stomach. As Mimnermos of Colophon observed in the 6th century BC: 'When painful old age overtakes a man and makes

EYEWITNESS

NEITHER YOUNG NOR OLD

THE ROMAN Babrios, living in the Greek-dominated eastern part of the empire in the 2nd century AD, comments on life in middle age:

❝ A man who was already "middle aged" – he wasn't a young man any more, nor as yet an elderly one, but his white and black hairs were mixed up together – was still devoting his time to love affairs and carousing. He was sleeping with two women, one a girl, the other an old woman. The girl wanted him to look like a young lover, the old woman like someone of her own age. The one who was in her prime plucked out the hairs which she found that were turning white, while the old woman plucked out any black ones she came across. This state of affairs lasted until the two women bequeathed to one another a bald pate, having plucked out all his hairs. ❞

him ugly outside and foul-minded within, then wretched cares eat away at his heart and no longer does he rejoice to gaze upon the sun, being hateful to young men and despicable to women. Such a grievous affliction has the god made old age.'

Folktales portrayed ageing as, at best, a burden on humankind and, at worse, a positively evil force. The mythological Geras, personification of old age, was believed to have been born of Night along with siblings such as Doom, Fate, Death and other unattractive characters. On the other hand, there were some more positive views of old age, as was shown by Xenophon. According to him, 'beautiful old men' were chosen to 'carry olive shoots in honour of Athene' during the annual All-Athenian Festival (Panathenaea) – which, he commented, 'shows that beauty is the accompaniment of every age'.

On the whole, it was the appearance of old women rather than old men that provoked artists' and writers' disgust. Spinsters inspired common revulsion among the ancient Greeks – many of the most horrendous figures in their mythology (including Medusa and the Furies) are spinsters. Every existing vase

FAIR OF FACE Even the youth-besotted Greeks acknowledged that some old men were imposing enough to play a key role at religious festivals.

47

painting which portrays an old woman does so, at best, as pathetic and, at worst, as some sort of monster. The playwright Aristophanes also tapped this prejudice in his vitriolic portrayals of old women in his later comedies. Here, they are depicted as oversexed old hags in pursuit of young men. Theatrical masks used, mostly in comedy, to denote various kinds of old women included the wrinkled old woman, the she-wolf, the obese old woman and the sharp-tongued old woman. Sometimes old men are also grotesquely evoked on vase paintings where they appear as lustful old satyrs chasing beautiful girls who are trying to escape them. According to the philosopher Theophrastros, in the 4th century BC, elderly flashers were a constant public nuisance.

THE FACE OF DOTAGE
This bronze mask illustrates some of the contempt Athenians felt for old age.

By the 4th century BC, the Athenians had become famous in the Greek world for their disrespect towards the elderly, which contrasted notably with the reverence the Spartans showed for their old people. This attitude had its critics, even in Athens. Xenophon asked: 'When will the Athenians respect their elderly the way the Spartans respect theirs instead of despising everyone older than themselves, beginning with their own fathers?'

The historian Herodotus noticed that only the Spartans got to their feet when an older man came in the room. And Plutarch tells the story of an old Athenian searching for somewhere to sit at the theatre who had to wait until a visiting Spartan vacated his seat for him. The Athenians seeing this courteous act loudly applauded it, at which the Spartan remarked to his companion: 'These Athenians certainly know how to recognise good manners, but not how to put them into practice.'

Athenian boys and girls had little contact with their fathers, and as teenaged boys wandered the city in bands of the same age groups. In contrast, Spartan children were always strictly supervised by their elders and were taught reflex obedience to them from the beginning. This attitude was also embodied in their government structure. The chief governing body in Sparta, known as the Gerousia, was made up of the two

PEER-GROUP BONDING **Outside their homes, these young Athenian boys would have little contact with their elders.**

hereditary kings, together with 28 men of 60 or over 'who were judged to be outstanding in virtue'. The Gerousia was empowered to enforce the death penalty and it was this awesome power, according to Xenophon, that accounted for the Spartans' habit of showing more respect for the elderly.

WELFARE FOR THE ELDERLY

In Athens, there was no state support for the elderly beyond a few handouts of corn, distributed to the needy in times of famine, and pensions for those whose sons had died at war. At the same time, Greek literature mentions none of the social issues nowadays associated with old age: loneliness, cold or hunger. Their physical and mental decline were also largely ignored.

The care of old people fell entirely on their families, with some households supporting as many as three or four generations of kinspeople. The elderly relations were expected to earn their keep by contributing as far as they were able to the household's prosperity.

It was also a matter of pride for elderly Greeks to demonstrate that they were not entirely defunct. Writers frequently criticise elderly layabouts: Plato, who normally showed a profound respect for the elderly, was none the less contemptuous of those who gave up an active life for 'the domesticity that befits women'. He argued that in old age people possessed both the leisure and the wisdom to contribute to the government of the state. Certainly Athenians were never too old for public office: the statesman Phokion in the 4th century BC was elected general 45 times and was only deprived of the post when he was 80.

In Athens, rich men without any children of their own adopted heirs, as 'the only refuge against isolation and the only possible consolation in life for childless persons', according to the orator Isaeus. An adopted son was expected to care for his foster-father while the older man was still alive and to bury him properly when he died. In such cases, the law decreed that the adopted son should

OLD AGE   A couple on a 5th-century BC drinking cup are shown with distorted heads and bodies.

relinquish all bonds of kinship with his blood family to ensure that he entered into the contract with proper filial devotion.

For the elderly poor without fortunes to barter, the outlook was extremely grim. Old Athenian men could serve on juries for a nominal sum but even these pickings had to be sought in competition with everyone else who was 30 or over. Aristophanes' comedies in the 5th century BC give the impression of juries filled to capacity with cantankerous old men, but if they were monopolised in this way it was probably because suitable younger competitors for the job were away fighting the Peloponnesian War.

Impoverished, widowed women, meanwhile, had little likelihood of remarriage since no one would look at a woman past childbearing age. Even among younger women, remarriage was less common than for widowed men because of the common mistrust of stepmothers. These were usually depicted in Greek literature as 'cuckoo figures' who would oust the legitimate heirs from their nest in order to secure their own sons' inheritances. The state provided a pension for widows who had borne a son; otherwise they were thrown on the mercy of their husbands' relations. Postmenopausal women at least had the option of trying out the profession of midwife, and a handful of cult rituals were confined

THE AGE OF PHILOSOPHERS

Thinkers from Socrates onwards delved deep into life's mysteries,

laying the groundwork, as they did so, for much of Western culture.

SOCRATES was about 70 when he died drinking hemlock on the orders of the hostile Athenian authorities. Plato died aged about 80; Aristotle was a relatively youthful 62 at his death. The three most elevated thinkers of Greek philosophy were living proof that advancing years and intellectual, if not physical, vigour were fully compatible.

Socrates, born in Athens around 470 BC, was the earliest of the three. A short, ugly man with pop eyes and a fat snub nose, he nevertheless possessed immense moral authority. He proved his valour by fighting as a hoplite during the Peloponnesian Wars. At home, he pursued an austere style of life, though he could also be excellent company with friends such as the statesman Pericles, Pericles' consort Aspasia and Alcibiades.

Socrates never committed himself to paper and everything we know about him comes from Plato and another disciple, Xenophon. From Xenophon's account he emerges as a pragmatic man intent on finding commonsense solutions to practical problems – although from an unconventional angle. One Aristophanes (not the playwright) is dismayed to find himself the sole supporter of a stream of female relations during the Peloponnesian War. Socrates advises him to set them to work spinning and weaving for the market in contravention of the social norms. Plato, meanwhile, was concerned with Socrates'

mind rather than with the man. He recorded his conversations as elaborate logical confections in which the questioner is reduced to monosyllables after the master has used his enquiries as launching pads for his own exposition.

Like Socrates, Plato was an Athenian, related on his mother's side to the lawgiver Solon and belonging on his father's side to a family that claimed descent from no less a figure than the sea god Poseidon. After his teacher's execution in 399 BC, the 30-year-old Plato went with some fellow Socratics into temporary exile, travelling in the Greek islands, Egypt and Italy. After returning to Athens, he founded his famous Academy in 387. In writings such as *The Republic*, Plato used Socratic-style 'dialogues' to try to define absolutes, including Truth, Beauty and Goodness. This was in opposition to the Sophists who argued that concepts such as Justice were often a matter of mere expediency. Plato taught that access to these verities could be attained only by an elite equipped with superior mental faculties who must dedicate their lives to an elaborate intellectual training.

Politically, Plato was a magnificent but impractical dreamer. His pupil Aristotle – a Greek doctor's son from Stagirus in Macedonia

ABSTRACTED An unknown Greek philosopher raises his hand to his chin in reflective pose.

who entered Plato's Academy as a 17-year-old in 367 BC and spent the next 20 years there – criticised him for writing about unrealisable Utopias. Aristotle began describing the world as it was. He developed a system of logic and a terminology that would be the bedrock of philosophy for 1000 years to come. He devoted much time to describing the natural world; he also expanded this scientific approach to the study of human beings and their institutions. One of his most famous pupils was the young Alexander the Great whom he tutored for three years during the future conqueror's teens.

Two offshoots of Socrates' teaching were the Cynic and the Cyrenaic schools. The Cynics expanded upon the harsher side of Socratic teachings, maintaining that virtue was accessible only when man divorced himself from the material comforts of life – including family and friends. (The modern sense of cynic, meaning someone who expects the worst of human behaviour, is a corruption of the teachings of the Greek Cynics.) A famous example of Cynic philoso-

TUTORIAL **A mosaic shows Plato (seated with a stick) presiding at his Academy outside Athens.**

phy taken to an extreme was Aristotle's eccentric contemporary Diogenes who lived in a tub. The Stoics subsequently modified this teaching with the belief that people should learn to accept the things that happen to them with a calm, detached resolution.

The Cyrenaic school – named after the Greek city of Cyrene in North Africa where many of its adherents were born – adapted a Socratic doctrine by idealising the absence of vexation. Their beliefs were developed by Epicurus – born on Samos in 341 BC but moving to

Athens to found a school of philosophy in 306. He and his followers dedicated their lives to avoiding the stresses of ambition. The Cynics, Stoics, Cyrenaics and Epicureans were alike in believing in reason as the ultimate yardstick of life and the universe.

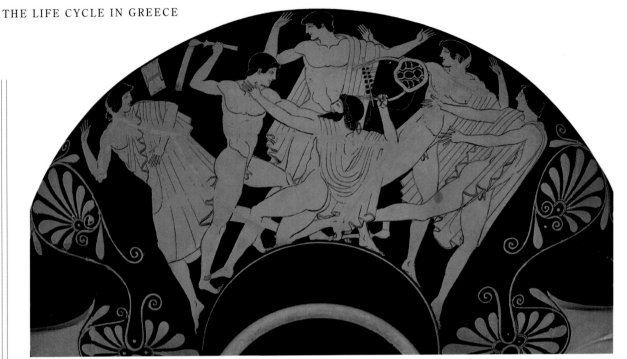

HEROIC THUGS A vase shows Heracles bludgeoning his elderly lyre-teacher to death with a broken chair leg.

to women beyond a certain age – the oracle at Delphi, for instance – but such positions were neither lucrative nor plentiful.

On the other hand, although the state offered little positive help to old people, it did come out strongly against the bad treatment of parents by their children. Before becoming a magistrate, a candidate had to swear that he had treated his parents well. It was illegal to deprive parents of sustenance, a roof over their head or a proper burial, or to beat them. These stipulations extended to grandparents and great-grandparents and were only nullified in the case of fathers who had failed to teach their sons a trade.

That the Greeks took an extremely dim view of those who ill-treated their parents is shown by the penalties meted out in a few specific cases: loss of all civic and political rights in Athens, for example, and a prison sentence for a child who failed to feed his parents in Delphi.

There was, however, a legal loophole for the maliciously disposed Athenian son. If he managed to convict his father of senility, the old man reverted to the

THERE'S LIFE IN THEM YET . . . Old age did not bring an end to all revelry. A stand from the early 5th century BC depicts old people dancing.

status of a child and forfeited all his civic and political rights, in which case he would be unable to bring a case of criminal neglect against his progeny. Nor did fathers have the power to disinherit their sons, unless a jury ruled that the father had been mistreated.

THE KEYS TO A LONG LIFE

The Greeks attributed a long life to some of the same factors that we do: the right kind of climate, diet and occupation, as well as innate physical and mental vitality, were all assumed to be life-prolonging.

The venerable ages many philosophers achieved were put down to their wisdom and to the good care they took of their health. The rhetorician Gorgias of Leontini in the 4th century BC, for instance, lived until he was 108, and attributed his longevity to the fact that he had never dined in anyone else's house and so had never succumbed to the temptation of overeating or of excessive drinking.

Aristotle believed that ageing was due to dehydration and decreasing body temperature. Thus

52

FAITHFUL TO THE END A 5th-century BC terracotta relief shows Penelope reunited with her husband Odysseus after his long adventures.

circumstances permitting, hoped to live until they were 70. The Athenian lawgiver Solon declared that a man who left life at this age could not be considered to have done so prematurely; he himself was said to have lived until he was 100.

The majority of elderly Greeks were active right up to the point at which they were struck down by their final illnesses, which were usually mercifully brief and painless. The Hippocratic oath, laying down the ethical code of the Hippocratic school of medicine on Cos, forbade doctors to practise euthanasia, stating that those who swore the oath were 'not to administer a poison to anybody when asked to do so and not to propose such course'. But the very fact that it was necessary to make such a stipulation suggests that mercy killings were practised. Many doctors who did not belong to the Hippocratic school would have had no moral compunction at all about ending the life of an incapacitated individual. Nevertheless, the belief that suicides and those who had died prematurely comprised a particularly unhappy group in Hades would probably have deterred all but the most desperate.

PREPARING FOR DEATH

An Athenian preparing for death might take the precaution of making a will. This could take the form of a written testimony which was read out to assembled relations, sealed and then consigned to the custody of trustworthy friends. Alternatively, the dying man would summon his relations to his bedside where, in the presence of two disinterested parties, he would announce his various wishes. In either case, the sick man would ensure that everyone with a possible claim on his property was

people who lived in hot climates lived longer than those in cold climates because they 'cool down' more gradually. In similar fashion men, who were believed to have hotter bodies than women, consequently had a greater life expectancy than the opposite sex. Aristotle also believed that too much sex was detrimental to health because sperm was moisture-retaining and therefore should not be expended capriciously.

Women tended to die sooner than men, probably because they gave birth to children so soon after puberty. In practice, few people of either sex lived until they were 65 because of war and epidemics. Yet the potential lifespan of the ancient Greek was no shorter than in our own times: a 4th-century BC gravestone records that the Athenian Euphranor of Rhamnus attained the great age of 105. The Greeks themselves, war and personal

AN ATHENIAN MOURNING THE PASSING OF HIS FATHER

FACES OF GRIEF
A 3rd-century BC
storage jar depicts
mourning figures.

THE DAY AFTER his father Demetrius died, Alexis was overcome by a feeling of detachment, as though he had left his body to look down on the activities of the household. There were his mother, grandmother and sister looking like ghouls in their black mourning clothes, their heads shorn of their long locks which they had worked into wreaths to place on the household altar.

As Alexis fingered his own newly shaved nape, he looked towards his father's body laid out in his bier. He had a coin in his mouth for journey money and a honeycake as an offering to the underworld gods. Everything was as it should be and yet it seemed a paltry affair to Alexis. Why did his father's body have to be secreted away like this, rather than being exposed in a public courtyard for public admiration, as his ancestors had been? The Homeric hero Hector, it was said, had

been on public display for a full nine days because the gods had intervened to slow his body's decomposition. Demetrius was not a hero, but he had still been famed for his courage in war and had been an exemplary citizen from a rich household.

Alexis's reverie was broken by his mother's sharp reminder that the vessel of purifying water should already be in place outside the entrance to warn passers-by of the pollution of death within. On the threshold, he met his uncle who had come to pay his respects. Soon the house was filled with wild laments from the old hags who deemed themselves friends.

The night drew on until the early hours of the morning, when it was time to wrap his father in a shroud and cover

his bier with a richly embroidered cloak. In silence, the members of the funeral cortege set out along the dark streets leading to the outskirts of the city where the family tomb lay.

They arrived at the tomb and the crematory pyre was torched. Alexis could make out the grave mound of his grandfather and grandmother in the flickering light. He listened to the speeches celebrating his father's virtues, while proceeding round the pyre with other mourners who were consigning gifts to the flames – he saw his mother-in-law throw on a piece of embroidered cloth. As he piled up the earth above his father's ashes and made sacrifices at the graveside, he noted how the simple marble slab caught the light from the dying embers of the fire. He was suddenly aware that he was too tired to go through the physical motions of eating and drinking at the feast the mourners would have at his home.

ASHES TO ASHES
The members of a family
parade around a
cremation pyre.

FROM HERE TO ETERNITY A corpse is prepared for burial in this fragment from an Attic vase of the 6th century BC.

present. Young Athenians preparing to go to war might make similar provisions.

The law stated that whoever disposed of a dead man's remains could make a bid for his property. This meant that someone who wished to put in a claim for a rich man's inheritance might try to hijack the burial ceremony. Sometimes there were unseemly squabbles at the graveside as the interested parties jockeyed for the spoils. In one recorded instance, a rich man called Nicostratus died abroad, and two soldiers claimed to have buried him. The problem was that because he was far from home, it was difficult to ascertain who his relations were. The whole of Athens, according to one account, was 'putting on mourning in the hope of being able to put in a successful claim'. In another court case, reported by the orator Isaeus, an old

man died in the house of his mistress; her sons tried to lay claim to his estate by attempting to prevent his legitimate wife from entering the household to perform the last rites for her husband.

In the 6th and 7th centuries BC, the funerals of the rich had reached such a degree of ostentation that the Athenian lawgiver Solon legislated to curtail their extravagance – at the time, the rapacity of the rich was causing social unrest. He stipulated an upper expenditure, outlawed all lamentation except within the home and at the graveside and restricted the number of mourners who might attend. He also banned the practice of hiring professional female mourners who had previously howled their laments at every street corner on the way to the ceremony. Furthermore, the corpse was to be buried with no more than three robes for its future use.

The restrictions on mourning also served to control the feuds between families that were a constant threat to the stability of the state. In an age when, if a man had been killed, his family frequently took revenge into their own hands, the funeral was often a highly charged affair designed to arouse their vengeful ire. The result was endless vendettas that the authorities did their best to control by setting up courts of law, to making binding judgments between the various parties, and an official damping down of the mourning sessions.

DEATH'S COSTUME JEWELS Personal ornaments, such as this 4th-century BC necklace of gilded terracotta, were buried with the dead.

ETERNITY AND THE AFTERLIFE

The various mystery cults that flourished at times in ancient Greece, involving their adherents in secret and often complex initiation rites, offered the initiates the prospect of some sort of paradise after death. For most people, however, death meant a miserable existence as wraiths dwelling timelessly in Hades. The dead person drank from the river of forgetfulness (Lethe) and consequently had no past or future but only a timeless present.

The torments of Hades were endlessly repetitive. One famous example of such suffering was Tantalus, a legendary king who had offended the gods, according to one account, by stealing their nectar and ambrosia and offering them to humans. In Greek myth, his punishment was to spend eternity hankering after the food and drink that was always before him but just out of his reach. He stood up to his neck in water whose level fell the moment he tried to drink from it, while fruits hanging over his head were whisked away by the wind

WATER FOR THE DEAD Special vases held water with which mourners washed the dead person's body.

if he grabbed at them. Sisyphus, a trickster king of Corinth, perpetually pushed a stone up a hill which then always rolled down again. The Danaids, the 50 legendary daughters of Danaus, King of Argos, who killed their husbands on their wedding night, tried to fill a punctured bucket with water.

Given the less than blissful existence of these wraiths, it seems surprising that an improper burial was considered an even worse fate. But in the *Iliad*, when the dead Patrocolus appears to his friend Achilles who is determined to avenge his death, the dead man is much more interested in being consigned to earth as quickly as possible. This, rather than revenge, is what he pleads for before vanishing with a thin shriek.

The cult of the dead played a vital part in the lives of surviving relations. On the third day after a funeral, the dead person's kinsfolk would make a pilgrimage to the cemetery where they offered libations and sacrifices to the deceased, followed by a feast for the family; such pilgrimages were repeated annually on the anniversary of the person's death. Athens also had a kind of 'remembrance day', the Genesia, each year, in which those who had died in war were honoured.

An Athenian law forbade people to worship at the tombs of those who were unrelated to them, other than at their funerals. This prevented them from ingratiating themselves with rich friends by attending to their dead kin and from displaying too much loyalty to any particular powerful family rather than the state. Where permitted, the libations of wine and milk and food offerings – salt, cakes, fruit – were put into specially designed bowls with pierced bottoms so that sustenance could percolate down into the earth where the

THE IMPORTANCE OF A PROPER TOMB

FAMILY GRIEF A grave relief commemorates an Athenian lady, Ampharete, and her dead grandchild.

BY THE 5TH century BC, every Athenian citizen had a tomb in which his dead relations were buried. These tombs were extremely important to him: aspiring office-holders, for instance, had to satisfy existing officials that they knew where 'their tombs' were. This was part of extensive questioning about their kinship groups and rights to Athenian citizenship.

In Athens, the main cemetery lay on either side of the main road leading from the city to the Academy where Plato established his school. It was here that the state provided a common tomb for soldiers killed in action. Other burial grounds existed on family estates. These grave plots were surrounded by low stone walls in the 5th century and developed into monumental tomb enclosures in the 4th century. They usually comprised three or four graves – at most half a dozen – each of which might house several family members as well as their slaves.

Before the 5th century BC, elaborate sculptured reliefs advertised the courage and virtuous deeds of warrior-aristocrats to anyone who passed by, while inscriptions requested strangers to pray for the dead men in honour of their achievements. But as part of the drive to curb ostentatious funerals, it was ruled that no grave monument could be more elaborate than the work ten men could finish in three days. Nor could tombs be marked with standing stones or adorned with painted plaques. Instead, Athenians had to content themselves with oil vases depicting the monuments they would have liked to erect.

When more elaborate monuments were reintroduced at the beginning of the Peloponnesian War in 431 BC, they had a new, more domestic emphasis, with women and children appearing on them for the first time. One surviving monument shows a woman sitting beside a nurse tending her child; another has a small child trailing a kind of go-cart and embarking on Charon's boat that will ferry him to the underworld. Even when a dead man is shown as a soldier, he is saying farewell to his wife and children as a living member of the family circle. Sometimes, it is hard to know who has actually died because the stones were often erected in anticipation of the deaths of other family members who would eventually be buried in the same plot. From the late 5th century, the impression created by the stones is private and unheroic, with the virtues of all members of the family now being celebrated. 'What a good girl you were! Dionysia is praised by her husband Antiphlos for loving him . . . more than clothes and jewellery', reads one inscription from around 350 BC, while another tells us that the parental nickname for a dead little boy was 'chatterbox'. On another stone, a dead wife greets her living husband requesting him to 'kiss my family for me'. Slaves, meanwhile, had to make do with truncated columns on which their names alone were inscribed.

dead person lay. At home, a statue or picture of the dead person was kept beside a household altar.

For the wraiths in Hades, it was a fate worse than death itself to be deprived of such remembrance rituals. People could be expected to live on only in the memory of their descendants, so that the maintenance of family tombs was a solemn duty – rich men sometimes freed slaves to tend their masters' graves. At the Battle of Salamis in 480 BC, at which the Greeks defeated the Persians, the most potent patriotic rallying cry called on the Greek soldiers to fight in order to free their land, their ancestral tombs and the temples of their gods. Their lands, their ancestral tombs and their temples were also what many country people were reluctant to abandon when Spartan invasions during the Peloponnesian War forced them to retreat inside the city walls of Athens. Family tombs also established one's citizenship: in Athens, for example, candidates for the post of magistrate were asked if they possessed family tombs and where these were – all as part of a process of checking that they were indeed proper citizens.

GUARDIANS OF THE UNDERWORLD Persephone, Queen of Hades, stands on the right of this 5th-century BC relief (above). A fearsome-looking Cerberus (below), guardian of the gates of Hades, is held back by his keeper.

LIFE IN THE GREEK HOME

The Greeks had little time for creature comforts, reserving their architectural
genius for temples and gods. Their own homes were mostly small, dark and
unsanitary. The poorest lived in lean-to shacks; the richest built
relatively modest two-storey houses around a courtyard, with segregated
quarters for men and women. Bathrooms and kitchens were rare –
most people cooked outside and ferried in water from public fountains.

LIFE IN THE CITY

Everywhere was within walking distance in cities such as Athens. Men congregated

in the market or made their way up to the sacred Acropolis to commune with

the gods. Each craft monopolised a different area within the city.

A MODERN traveller flying into Athens from the west has a good aerial view of the mountains that cover at least four-fifths of Greece. All across the country they divide one small plain from another and extend in convoluted chains that at ground level dominate the horizon. In ancient Greece they were covered with bush and scrub, and in the north forests of plane trees and oaks. Here, rare Nemean lions occasionally prowled, though stags and wild boar, both favourite prey for hunters, were much more common.

Cities grew up where groups of scattered villages merged on the lowest foothills of the mountains and in the plains. Only there was the soil rich enough to cultivate crops. The city was the focal point of a much more extensive agricultural area that also formed part of the Greek city-state or polis. Generally, these rural hinterlands were small because the Greeks lacked resources to develop them on a large scale. Athens was exceptional in being the urban centre of a large polis embracing the whole of Attica, approximately the same size as modern-day Luxembourg and marginally bigger than Rhode Island – 965 sq miles (2500 km^2). Elsewhere, a polis might monopolise an entire island, but the island of Lesbos, for instance, comprised five separate city-states.

People who lived in the country and those who lived in the city were bound by the same laws, meaning that farmers were as much a part of the polis as city-dwellers. Rich farmers might own both a country and a town house and divide their time between the city's bustle of commerce and culture and the peace of their farms. But for the less wealthy country-dwellers in areas such as Attica, rural towns and villages remained vibrant local centres with their own

markets, religious traditions and fairs. All these smaller Attic towns had strong identities: the fortified town of Eleusis, for example, was the centre of a famous mystery cult (a cult involving secret initiation) and regularly attracted thousands of its followers, while Akharnai, only a few miles from Athens, was the home of charcoal-burners who collected their wood from the slopes of the neighbouring Mount Parnes.

THE CITY ON HIGH AND THE PORT

Even cities were very small by modern standards. Before the Athenian Acropolis – measuring 1000 ft (300 m) by 500 ft (150 m) – became the precinct of the gods in the 5th century BC, it was the town itself, with the country extending right up to its walls. Even after it was set aside for the gods, each area of Athens was still within easy walking distance of the Acropolis.

The Athenian port of Piraeus was a fortified town in its own right. In contrast to the main city, it had been developed in systematic fashion in the early 5th century BC as a checkerboard of fine, straight streets lined with well-placed houses. It had pleasantly open areas allotted to public and business buildings, ranging from workshops to temples, dockyards to warehouses. Unlike the main city, there was also a strong racial mix with foreign traders lodging alongside resident aliens (metics). This mix produced a variety of shrines and temples that gave the port a cosmopolitan feel. According to Plato,

GODLY RESIDENTS Before it was given over to the gods, Athens' Acropolis (right) had been a residential area. Left: Vase painters, like this one, let their pots dry in the sun before applying the decoration.

A DAY AT THE GYM

THE PLAYWRIGHT Aristophanes extols the pleasures of exercising at the gymnasium in the Academy recreation ground that lay just outside Athens:

❛ Flower-fresh, oil-smooth, you will spend your time in the gymnasium. You will go down to the Academy, and there, under the sacred olives, crowded with a wreath of green reed, you will run a course against some decently behaved young man of your own age, redolent of woodbine, and happy unconcern, and deciduous white poplar, rejoicing in springtime, when plane and elm whisper together. ❜

BLOOD SPORT
A huntsman and his dog head out for some sport.

his mentor Socrates once descended to Piraeus to view the festival of the Thracian goddess Bendis: 'I wanted to say a prayer to the goddess and also to see what they would make of the festival, as this was the first time they were holding it.'

If a sailor arriving in the port wished to give thanks for his safe journey home, he could climb from Piraeus to the Acropolis along a passage nearly 7 miles (11 km) long. This was sheltered by the Long Walls, an extension of the city walls built between 461 and 450 BC to ensure that the seafaring Athenians would never be cut off from the sea. In peacetime, however, the sailor would probably prefer to use the adjacent main road.

After a long walk, he would arrive at the city's stone walls, rebuilt after the Persian wars towards the end of the 5th century BC by the combined effort of all Athenian citizens, including women and children. The new ramparts, which were wide enough to permit two wagons to meet and pass on top of them, enclosed an area that was roughly oval in shape. Towers provided defensive lookout posts and there were 14 gates.

SHOE SHINE An African slave boy cleans a boot. His would have been one of many foreign faces in the streets of Athens.

The main entrance was the Dipylon gate where three roads met: one from the south; another, 'the Sacred Way', which came from Eleusis and was bordered by cemeteries; and a third that led from the Academy, a public park north-west of the city. Inside the walls, the northern side of the city was dominated by the huge residential area of the Scambonidae, where most of the more prosperous citizens chose to live – it had its own two gates giving access to the countryside. The poor lived in areas lying to the south-west. On the eastern side, outside the walls, was a stretch of recreation ground.

If he was in a hurry to reach the Acropolis, a traveller would probably take the Panathenaic Way, the main road, which passed through the potters' quarter or Kerameikos. Alternatively, he might cut across the bronze-statue-making district. Finally, he would take the path leading up from the market place to the Acropolis. Once on top, he would find himself amidst a crowd of statues, altars and temples, some of them, like the Parthenon, huge and beautifully proportioned, others smaller and

TOWNS BY THE GRID

The idea of laying out towns on a grid system originated with the ancient Greeks. The Athenians hired Hippodamus of Miletus – a philosopher whose special subject was geometry – to develop the Piraeus port area of their city. He devised a plan in which all the streets cut one another at right angles, dividing the town into square or rectangular districts.

STREET TRADE An Athenian sculptor chips away at a figurine. Country people wander past, some of them heading for the Acropolis rising in the background.

older. As he wandered among them, he might see a thin plume of smoke rising where someone was sending up an offering.

Looking out over the edge of the Acropolis, he would see the six other hills the Athenians had appropriated to themselves including, to the west, the lower Hill of the Pnyx where the Assembly gathered and the Hill of Ares where the old aristocratic council had met before democracy developed. Beneath him, he would see the city's huddle of

houses, divided by a network of streets all of which, in contrast to the more ordered splendour of the Acropolis, had evolved haphazardly and without forethought.

BUSTLE IN THE MARKETPLACE

The marketplace (Agora) was the heart of the main city. Here, the garrulous Athenians gathered to chat, conduct personal or civic business and buy or sell produce through barter or cash exchange.

RISING FROM THE ASHES: REBUILDING THE ACROPOLIS

BETWEEN THEM, the statesman Pericles and sculptor Pheidias brought Athens' Acropolis back to life. For 30 years since the Persians razed Athens in 480 BC, the precinct of the gods had been left in a pitiable state as a reminder of their aggression. Then Pericles hired Pheidias to supervise its rebuilding. Crisp, white marble was quarried from Mount Pentelikon north-east of Athens and fashioned by the most skilled craftsmen of the day.

The crowning glory was the Parthenon, dedicated to Athena Parthenos ('the Maiden'). For a structure of such complexity, it was built at speed – between 447 and 432 BC – over the foundation of its predecessor. No mortar was used, with the marble blocks fastened by iron clamps instead. Standing on a platform of three steps, a series of Doric columns (with plain capitals and no base) tapered upwards. Inside, above a second set of columns, was a magnificent frieze. The large east door allowed the strong morning sunlight to illuminate the great gold and ivory statue of Athena inside (sculpted by Pheidias himself).

After the Parthenon, the craftsmen moved on to the Acropolis' entrance gate, the Propylaea. Having passed through the central entrance into a porch, pilgrims' eyes would have been drawn upwards by three Ionic columns (with a base and ram's-horn capitals) to richly sculpted ceiling panels picked out in shades of gold, blue, green and red.

The Propylaea was bordered on one side by a gallery hung with pictures of mythical scenes, and on the other by the small Temple of Athena Nike ('Bringer of Victory'). On the left stood the Erechtheum, an elaborate building that contrasted with the Parthenon's simple lines. It housed an ancient wooden statue of Athena that had greater religious importance for the Athenians than Pheidias' marvellous work in the Parthenon. It was to pay homage to this crude old image that the Panathenaic Procession wended its way across the city each year.

FINISHING TOUCHES   Painters work on the Parthenon frieze and pediments, adorning the sculptures in gaudy hues.

YOUTHS ON HORSEBACK A frieze from the Parthenon shows scenes from the annual Panathenaic procession.

It was surrounded by many of the city's principal public buildings. There were, in particular, four colonnaded walkways (stoas). The first, the Stoa of the Herms, was constructed over and around several Herms (rough stone blocks carved with the face of the god Hermes and his exaggerated genitals). It was a favourite meeting place for young cavalrymen, the offspring of wealthy families who served as cavalry in wartime. A cavalry contest started and finished here during the annual Panathenaic (All-Athenian) festivities. At other times of the year, the cavalrymen might occupy their time by talking to notable figures such as Socrates.

The second stoa called the Stoa Poikile ('the painted stoa') was built in about 460 BC and took its name from a series of painted plaques by the well-known Athenian artists Polygnotos, Mikon and Panainos. It was here that juries often met to arbitrate in legal disputes.

A third stoa, the Royal Stoa, was where newly elected officials stood on a block of stone to give their oath that they would abide by the state's laws. Inside the colonnade stood marble slabs on which citizens could read the 'Laws of Solon', which had reformed the city's constitution in the 6th century BC.

The fourth colonnade, an imposing structure of the late 5th century BC, was dedicated to Zeus. It was one of Socrates' favourite haunts. Next to it were the Council House (where council members met and took their meals) and the Round Building, where the council's different subcommittees, each responsible for running the city's affairs for a month, were on permanent call during their period of duty. Opposite was a fenced pedestal with statues of the ten tribal heroes of Attica. This was also used as a public noticeboard to display details of proposed legislation and imminent lawsuits and lists of men called up for military service.

Surrounded by these grand buildings, the daily markets proceeded noisily under the shade of plane trees. The comic poet Euboulos in the 4th century BC summarised the variety of business transacted: 'You will find everything sold together in the same place at Athens: figs, witnesses to summonses,

BIRD OF THE GODDESS
An Athenian coin shows an
owl – Athena's special bird.

UP FROM THE COUNTRY
A figurine shows a woman
riding sidesaddle on a mule.

bunches of grapes, turnips, pears, apples, givers of evidence, roses, medlars, porridge, honeycombs, chickpeas, lawsuits. . . .'

Every inch of available space was crammed with booths and workshops, since most customers preferred to do their shopping in the Agora, rather than taking the trouble to go to the various outlying districts that were dedicated to each of the different trades.

Peasants, who had walked in from the country, arrived at dawn carrying vegetables, oil in pots and other agricultural produce that they would sell to the city-dwellers. While they were there they would also acquire city produce for themselves and hear first-hand accounts of the affairs of the state. Sometimes, particularly during the festival of the Great Dionysia at the end of March, there would be foreign visitors, most of them from city-states that were part of Athens' empire.

All these people, the richer ones accompanied by slaves who would later carry their purchases home for them, had to make their way through the market's obstacle course of makeshift shops and stalls, most of them little more than clapboard huts with skin or wattle roofs. But what appeared to be

PICKING AND CHOOSING A shopper
inspects the goods before negotiating
a deal. He will pay using either barter
or small-denomination currency.

PERFECT FIT A cobbler on this Attic vase prepares to cut out a leather sole using his customer's foot as a template.

chaos had an underlying order. Like a modern Middle Eastern souk, each stall was grouped with others selling similar merchandise and Athenians all knew their way around them. So they knew that one corner of the market was reserved for booksellers, another for sellers of kitchen equipment (some kitchen items were also available for hire) and in another place you could buy oil. Here you could purchase a myrtle wreath for a funeral, and over there some make-up. Each stall or shop was called after the thing it sold; as a character from an anonymous fragment of comedy says: 'I went round to the garlic and the onions and the frankincense and the perfume.'

There were always different things to look out for. A cobbler named Simon kept shop in his house on a corner of the Agora. Lamps or cereals might be bought from stalls in the colonnades. Bankers like Pasion – an ex-slave who went on to make himself a fortune lending money – found it more convenient to sit behind tables. Labourers who wished to hire themselves out gathered near the Temple of Hephaistos. Shopping for slaves involved a journey

to an area near the shrine of Dioskouroi on the slopes of the Acropolis.

Barber shops were notorious centres of gossip, while at the fishmongers' citizens would watch carefully in case these famously dishonest vendors tried to cheat them by saturating their produce in water to make it seem heavier than it was.

Ten annually elected measure-controllers patrolled the booths to ensure that tradespeople used the standardised weights and measure. The responsibilities of another group of ten ranged from preventing waste dumping within the market place to stopping housebuilders from obstructing the streets with building material or overhanging gutters. They also checked up on flute girls or prostitutes to make sure they were not charging exorbitant amounts.

Sometimes, the Agora was cleared for state occasions. One of the most important of the city's annual festivals, the Panathenaic Procession for instance, passed diagonally across it on its way to the Acropolis, and crowds gathered on stands to witness the *continued on page 70*

LIFE IN THE CITY CENTRE

SCAMPERING dogs and children mingle with the buyers and sellers in a city marketplace or agora. Jars on their heads, women make for a fountain to collect water – a task that enabled even the most respectable housewives to venture out of doors and meet their friends.

The agora was the hub of city life. Here, farmers came in from the country to sell fruit, vegetables and cheeses to the city-dwellers. Other stalls sold fish and pottery, scent bottles and caged birds. Shoemakers plied their trade; an orator on a pedestal might be plying his. Colonnaded buildings known as stoas lined the sides of the agora, offering shade where friends met to discuss local affairs and exchange news.

AT THE WATER FOUNTAIN Fetching water gave women one of their few opportunities to leave the home.

great event. It was also in the Agora that the practice of ostracism was carried out. This was a device to prevent the city from splitting into factions. If two rival politicians were dividing the citizens, an ostracism was held to determine which one should leave Athens for ten years, his property being left intact for that time. An area in the Agora was enclosed by a fence with ten doors (one for each of the ten tribes), and each citizen entered through the relevant door to deliver, on a fragment of pot, the name of the man he wished to be evicted.

POTHOLES AND MUDSLIDES

Once shoppers had completed their business and sent their slaves ahead with their purchases, they returned home for the midday meal because the

---

EYEWITNESS

WHEN STATESMEN LED CIRCUMSPECT LIVES

THE ATHENIAN orator and soldier Demosthenes (384-322 BC) contrasted the corrupting ostentation of 4th-century politicians with the simpler lifestyles of their 5th-century predecessors:

❛ [Statesmen in the old days] led circumspect private lives, and their behaviour conformed to the traditions of our city: so much so that . . . the houses of men such as Aristides or Miltiades or any other famous citizen of those times were in no way more distinguished than their neighbours . . . Today, I am told, our public life may be somewhat in decline, but our civic amenities are vastly improved. What proof of such an assertion have we? Trumpery details such as repointed parapets on the city walls, or repairs to fountains, or newly surfaced roads. Take a good look at the men who implement this kind of policy. Some have jumped from poverty to affluence, others from obscurity to the highest public honours. Some have built themselves houses that outshine our public edifices; and indeed their fortunes have risen in proportion as those of the city have declined. ❜

MARKET TRADE An Attic black-figured cup of around 530 BC shows a merchant balancing his scales.

market closed at midday. The roads they walked along were lined with dilapidated houses forming a shambolic contrast with the fine buildings around the Agora and on the Acropolis.

Although a few luxuriously appointed houses existed in Athens, most 5th-century Greeks preferred to lavish their money on public buildings rather than risk divine wrath by demonstrating the sin of pride through private ostentation. Obviously, the rich quarter was much more presentable than the teeming part of the city occupied by tradespeople and the poor. Even though the city had been considerably improved since the 5th century, a traveller in the 2nd century AD had this to say about its less prosperous parts: 'The city of Athens is very drought-ridden: its water supplies are inadequate, and being so ancient a town it is badly planned. A stranger, coming on it unawares, might well doubt whether this could be the city of the Athenians.'

The roads, too, were in a terrible state, despite the efforts of special state officials to improve them. With the exception of the Panathenaic Way and the Street of the Tripods, which ran from the Agora around the eastern and western sides of the Acropolis, unpaved streets became progressively narrower as they twisted and turned up the hills. Houses were thoughtlessly built – some far back from the road, others encroaching onto it. Passers-by had to be wary of buckets

of evil-smelling slops thrown out of doors and windows. The slops then combined with water escaping from private cisterns to turn the tracks into potholed mudslides in rainy weather. In such conditions, it was hardly surprising that the Great Athenian Plague of 430 BC spread through the city like wildfire.

There were no street lights, either, to illuminate the way home for men who had drunk too much at dinner with friends. The jurymen in Aristophanes' play *The Wasps*, obliged to make their way to court before dawn, circumnavigate the mud holes with the help of slave boys carrying lamps before them.

The Boule (Council), which was responsible for public expenditure, had to appoint several subgroups of civil servants to try to address the different problems. Ten officials (five for Athens and five for Piraeus) were given the task of forming a police force and maintaining public works; another subgroup of road surveyors had a pool of slave labour at its disposal; and there was also a chief architect, though his powers were limited to the maintenance of temples and other civic buildings.

Lack of water was another constant concern in this arid country. The succession of tyrants who ruled Athens in the 6th century BC had provided the city with several fountains fed by underground pipes that brought in water from outside. The 'fountain with nine mouths' in the Agora was the biggest. By the 4th century, there was a special official in charge of the water supply. He was an important man, elected to the job rather than being chosen by lot as was customary with lesser office-holders. An Athenian decree in 333 BC celebrates one Supervisor of Fountains, a man named Pytheas, 'for having zealously acquitted himself in the performance of all his duties; and in particular for having completed the new fountain beside the Sanctuary of Amphiaraus, where he has ensured constant water and adequate drainage'. He was rewarded with a golden crown worth 1000 drachmas, and it seems that he was responsible for fountains throughout Attica since the Sanctuary of Amphiaraus was on the Boeotian border in the west.

EQUAL SHARE Officials used standard measures like these to ensure fair trading in the market.

LIFE IN THE HOME

Household management was the women's responsibility, although the men did

the shopping. At home the women cooked, made clothes, supervised the store

cupboards and ensured that the slaves performed their designated chores.

THE GREEKS had very little interest in domestic comfort, an attitude that was rooted in the harshness of their past. For men, life was lived outside – in the fields or streets – and they came home only to eat and sleep; women (except for those belonging to the very poorest families, who had to go out to work) spent the day at home.

To indulge in luxurious living was seen as a sign of decadent pride, and was carefully avoided by those wishing to succeed in political life. Thus a foreign traveller visiting Athens in the 3rd century BC noted that 'only one or two [homes] reach a decent standard of comfort'. Some of the most impoverished homes were simply caves cut out of the rock face. In the quarter dubbed The Hollow, where the Long Walls joined the city walls, one such dwelling consisted of three rooms together with a lean-to passageway at the entrance. Others were constructed against a squared-off rock face, or else built on small stepped ledges.

More substantial homes were generally single-storey buildings with rooms grouped around a central courtyard. The poorest had just two or three small rooms. The walls were usually made of wood, fired brick or stones glued together with mud. They were so flimsy that burglars, called 'wall piercers', simply knocked their way through them rather than going to the trouble of forcing windows or doors.

TAKING A BREAK
A mid-5th-century BC red-figure water jar shows a woman reading to three companions.

On one occasion, a notorious Athenian housebreaker known as Chalcous ('man of bronze') mocked the orator Demosthenes in the Assembly for the industrious late hours he kept. 'I am well aware that my late-burning lamp must be an embarrassment to you, Chalcous,' Demosthenes countered. 'And as for you, men of Athens, can you wonder that robbery is so rife, when thieves are brazen, and walls mere mud?' Many Greek city houses were terraced, which proved useful for the people of Plataea in Boeotia (bordering Attica to the west). When attacked by the Thebans in 431 BC, they burrowed through the party walls to assemble in secret.

Altogether houses were so shabbily made that landlords in Athens could easily dismantle them – taking off the roof tiles and front door – to dislodge tenants unable to pay their rent. Such unfortunates joined the tramps who slept in the city's bathhouses at night. Some of them got too close to the furnace and burnt themselves, prompting a character in a play by Aristophanes to ask Poverty: 'What good can you bring us except burns from the baths?'

LIFE ON THE INSIDE

Inside the home the rooms faced onto the courtyard, which helped to keep them cool in summer. Doors opened outwards and, according to the historian Plutarch, people customarily rapped on them before leaving a room as a warning to any passer-by on the other side. Windows were no more than small holes cut into the walls.

There were few large buildings, even in cities such as Athens. The nearest equivalents to modern high-rise blocks were two-storey buildings rented out to many tenants. A prosperous household in an upper-class district might also have a second storey for the strictly segregated women's quarters. One Athenian litigant who accused his wife of conducting an adulterous affair said that he had exchanged his ground-floor rooms for his wife's first-floor quarters to allow her to bathe their newborn child without risk of falling down the stairs each time she needed to visit the bathroom. Thus, in his innocence, he had enabled her to carry on her illicit liaison from the ground floor.

Food was generally cooked on braziers. In winter, when a fire was needed for warmth as well as cooking, poorer citizens would construct a makeshift air vent using a pole to push out one of the roof tiles, or they might make a hole under the cornice. This allowed them to do their cooking inside. Such rudimentary ventilation meant that the atmosphere inside most homes was dark and choking, particularly in bad weather when the window holes were covered over in order to keep the rain out. In rich households with proper kitchens the fire was normally kindled outside and then brought into the kitchen when the embers in the brazier were red-hot. Some of these wealthier homes also had clay 'smoke conduits', but they were rarely particularly effective.

DOMESTIC COMFORT This wealthy family has a two-storey home including a male dining room and extensive female quarters.

LIFE IN THE WOMEN'S QUARTERS

INDUSTRIOUS SCENE A woman prepares wool for the spinners while her companions weigh the fleeces. The epinetron (right) was placed on the lap and used by the women to prepare the wool for spinning.

CONFINED TO the upper storey or back part of a house, women were sometimes quite literally barred from the male quarters. This was to keep them safe from unwelcome contact with men who were not related to them. In their own quarters, however, they often enjoyed warm relationships with their husbands, even if the ideal was always that of secluded industriousness.

'Your business will be to stay indoors', the Athenian Xenophon told young wives categorically. Duties included ensuring that the outdoor slaves were dispatched promptly about their tasks and that the work of the household slaves was closely supervised. The housewife would receive all incoming money and use it to run the household while carefully watching over any surplus. Keeping the store cupboard well supplied was her responsibility – in particular, she had to ensure that any grain was kept dry. Xenophon also recommended kneading dough and shaking out bed covers and cloaks as good exercise.

Apart from the preliminary washing of sheep's fleeces in the courtyard, the entire process of spinning, weaving and making clothes was carried out in the women's quarters. It would be a cosy scene inside the room while all this took place, if dark and smelly by modern standards. Wife, mother-in-law, unmarried sisters of the head of the household and little girls would all be hard at work, while pre-school boys amused themselves as best they could.

The washed fleeces were beaten out on a bench to rid them of any impurities and then the wool was straightened into hanks for spinning and the hanks placed in a basket. Sitting on chairs or stools, or standing up, the women pulled the wool away from the distaff (the stick holding the unspun wool) with a spindle weighted with small flywheels known as whorls. Weaving was done on a loom – a large wooden frame on which the threads hung down with weights on the ends. A wooden shuttle that wove the horizontal thread through the vertical was thrown across from one side to the other.

The wool used might be dyed or left plain. The decorations were woven in at the loom and usually echoed the traditional motifs on Greek architecture and vases: key-pattern, battlements, rosebuds or lotus flowers. In the 5th century BC, some skilled weavers also began to work mythological scenes into their cloth – a fashion dubbed 'barbarian' because elaborate patterns on cloth were the hallmark of eastern weaves. Once the length of cloth was completed, the housewife packed it into wooden chests, possibly fashioned from contrasting shades of wood or ornamented with ivory inlays and bronze feet. Here, the cloth waited until its time came to be used as a cloak, wrap, blanket or curtain according to its size, thickness or design.

Women ate their meals sitting on chairs in their own quarters; men in wealthy households had special dining rooms where they entertained their friends in all-male dinner parties known as symposia. Apart from chairs and the couches used in the men's dining rooms and the occasional footstool, the principal household furnishings were chests and trunks used for storing clothes and jewellery.

Peasants rose at dawn and retired at dusk, and therefore had little need for any kind of artificial lighting. More prosperous citizens had olive-oil lamps. These were small and round and made of glazed clay, with a spout for a wick. They gave out a better light than the other form of artificial light, torches made of a branch or a few twigs. Rich households had lamps made of gold or silver.

All-male Entertainment

Wealthier men passed most of the little time they spent at home enjoying their symposia dinner parties. These gatherings were especially popular in Athens. At the start of such an evening, the guests would congregate in the porticoed court outside, where a fig tree might grow to give shade during the hot daylight hours.

On entering the dining room, the visitor's eye would immediately be drawn to the dresser opposite him (the Greeks did not have cupboards) with the household's precious cups and ornaments displayed on it. Around the walls were couches. At a dinner described by Plato, there was room for seven couches but other households could fit nine. The couches were wooden frames crisscrossed with webbing; on top of this lay a thin mat covered with a patterned rug that acted as a kind of mattress. The frames were decoratively carved and raised at one end, allowing the reveller to prop himself up on one arm, with the help of cushions. Each diner had a small, oblong, three-legged table in front of him

A GLIMPSE INTO THE HOME A woman puts some cloth away in a carved household chest. Hanging on the wall behind her are a basket, a mirror, a jar for oil and a two-handled goblet.

where slaves laid the individual servings of food brought in from the kitchen.

Above the couches were nails with more decorative cups hanging from them. Wreaths, long streamers of vine or ivy and sometimes tapestries decorated the otherwise plainly plastered walls. It was only at the beginning of the 4th century BC that painted murals started to appear – later in that century, they would become extremely elaborate. Alcibiades was rumoured to have imprisoned one decorator in his home for three months to ensure that he finished a fresco commission.

After a dinner, the host retired to bed, which in winter would be the same couch he had used for dining. He had a blanket with which to cover himself and a pillow for his head, but no sheets, which did not exist in ancient Greece. In the hot summer

MALE ENTERTAINMENT Torches
illuminate a richly decorated
male dining room. The feasters
reclined on the couches.

months, he was more likely to sleep out under the
stars on his roof, despite the fetid smells (not to
mention flees and lice) which pervaded insanitary
cities such as Athens.

FRUGAL FARE

In contrast to the symposia, everyday meals were
perfunctory affairs. Breakfast consisted of bread
dipped in wine. It was followed at midday by a
snack taken outdoors or at the corner of a table.
The final and most substantial meal of a normal
day was consumed equally unceremoniously in the
mid afternoon.

Although the rich lived well, fine cooking and
eating meant little to most ordinary people. Living
in a country with little cultivable land, for protein
they mainly ate goat's cheese, fish and some vegetables, indulging in occasional meat meals during

public sacrifices when animals were slaughtered for the gods. Theirs was a simple and extremely healthy diet, whose other principal ingredients were bread (consumed in vast quantities), a variety of broths, figs, olives and pulses cooked in olive oil. These foods were supplemented with a few herbs – thyme, marjoram and mint – cultivated or simply gathered from the wild, and the produce of the hunting bag, including hares, foxes and moles.

Although overeating was not generally a vice, there were some local variations. The people of Boeotia had a reputation for gluttony, which provoked the scorn of their fellows in other parts of Greece and was used to explain their supposedly thick-headed ways. At the other end of the scale, the Spartans existed on a particularly frugal diet, which included an infamous black broth made of pork, blood, salt and vinegar. The grammarian Athenaeus (writing around AD 200) recorded the story of a foreigner invited to dine in an all-male Spartan mess. As he ate he remarked that he had always been astonished by tales of the Spartans' courage but now he doubted the stories' truth: 'For any man in his senses would rather die 10 000 times over than live as miserably as this.'

Dishes tended to be high-tasting and rank-smelling – understandable enough in a world without refrigeration where food had to be stored to last throughout the winter months. The Greeks added honey to their food to balance, rather than obscure, its slightly rotten taste, just as the English combine Stilton with port or the Chinese harmonise sweet and sour tastes.

Cereals, essentially barley and wheat, which cities such as Athens had to import in large quantities from the area around the Black Sea, were often made into a kind of porridge flavoured with herbs. When making bread, women used stones to

HOMEWARD BOUND
Guests departing from a dinner party used lamps like this to light their way home.

BREAD TO SCOOP UP FOOD

Bread was an eating instrument as well as food, used to scoop up food into the mouth. Apart from knives, the Greeks had no other form of cutlery. Pitta-style bread was best for manipulating solid foods; larger round loaves were good for dunking in broths. At symposia dinner parties guests reclined on one arm, leaving the other free to ferry bite-sized morsels into the mouth.

grind the grain in wide, shallow troughs, and then pummelled the dough before putting it to bake in small portable pottery ovens. Wood fires were lit inside the ovens, then the hot ashes were raked to one side, the dough put in and a lid put on to conserve the heat.

Bread came in many forms, and different parts of the country were famous for particular kinds. Archestratus, a well-travelled Sicilian of Greek extraction, who wrote a long poem in celebration of gourmandise around 330 BC, singled out bread from the island of Lesbos for praise. It was so good that he commended it to the gods. He was similarly enthusiastic about the white bread from Erythrae, an Ionian city on what is now the west coast of Turkey, which 'comes out of the oven, bursting with the delicate flavours of the season'. He also liked 'Thessalian roll, rounded into a circle and well pounded by hand', but thought less of the bread from other parts of Greece, with the exception of the widely praised loaves and pastries on sale in the Athenian market.

He was, of course, exceptional in that most Greeks would not have had this extensive choice. The Athenian worker ate loaves made from cheap barley flour, while more prosperous citizens had the option of locally made wheat bread which came in round loaves.

For the ordinary man, garlic, onions and cheese added piquancy to a rather stodgy diet, especially in the army where those accustomed to more refined dishes at home complained of the indigestible and monotonous meals. Olives were plentifully available in most parts of Greece, although the Athenians suffered a shortage after the Spartans set fire to their orchards during the Peloponnesian War. The olives

GOOD HEALTH A drinking cup from the mid 4th century BC is shaped like a griffin's head.

were largely made into oil, which the Greeks used instead of butter, but were also eaten whole.

Peasants supplemented their diet with eggs, if they kept hens, as well as home-grown vegetables and small birds, snared in traps or nets, which they roasted over open fires or in small clay ovens. Other hot foods were prepared in small portable hearths using casseroles with lids (which could also be hired in the market) or a multipurpose rough jug which was used for heating water, soup or vegetables. Another cooking implement was the terracotta frying pan; for dry cooking, this was sometimes filled with hot embers with a fired-clay grill placed over them.

THE JOYS OF FISH

The main meal of the day might include fish. In the Athenian fish market, the most lively and colourful area in the Agora, a prosperous citizen might treat himself to an eel from Lake Copais in Boeotia, inspect the shellfish or shop for freshwater fish which were as popular as those from the sea. The 'boar fish', for instance, which skulked on riverbeds and was so named because of the grunting noise it made, was considered by Aristotle to be 'worth its weight in gold'. Squid, octopus and tuna, as well as big sea fish such as bass, were all netted for the rich man's table and eaten fresh or salted. Sturgeon was a luxury saltwater fish prized for its firm white flesh. For poorer people sardines were popular and any rise in their price provoked a panic among Athenian workers.

Good-quality fish was cooked simply, allowing full play to the natural flavours. It was sprinkled with salt and oil, usually with a dash of vinegar (the Greek equivalent of lemon) added to cut the fat. Indifferent or bad fish was disguised with the addition of strong ingredients, commonly cheese. The most luxurious fare might be served up on beautiful concave platters with fish painted around the rims. These allowed juices to run down into small indentations in the middle and mingle with the sauce.

A recipe mentioned by the travelling gourmand Archestratus of Sicily involved the elaborate preparation of a great parrotfish, which did include cheese although parrotfish was generally regarded as luxury fare: 'Prepare it whole as follows: cover completely with cheese and oil and hang in a hot oven. Then bake well. Sprinkle with salt mixed with cumin and yellow-grey oil, pouring down from your hand the god-given stream.' Using this method the fish juices would be retained by the cowl of cheese and oil but the fat would drip away leaving the flesh dry and ready for the addition of a superior table oil. Alternatively, a cook might wrap the fish in a fig or vine leaf tied up with rush cord and bake it in the fire embers or roast it in a tray and then serve the fish in its oily juices.

Salting fish was another art to which the Athenian Euthydemus dedicated an entire book. Fish such as mackerel and the famous Sicilian tuna were often treated in this way by soaking them in a salt solution (the length of time varying according to the type of fish). They were then stored in jars for easy transportation.

The 5th century BC saw a greater culinary divide open up between the rich and poor. Hors d'oeuvres came into vogue, cookery books appeared, and such delicacies as peacock's eggs became desirable. Although only a few fragments of cookery books survive from this time, it is clear that such exalted cuisine rarely included meat beyond the occasional dish of goose, a sow's womb prepared as a relish or roasted hare.

HARD LABOUR Women pound grain for bread making. Most people used barley – only the better-off could afford wheat.

AN ATHENIAN HOST AS HE GIVES A DINNER PARTY

CHARMIDES felt well prepared for his dinner in honour of his friend Callias. Callias had been living on his estate for three months, boasting that the country air and food would restore him to youth. In spite of himself, Charmides had been annoyed and had invited his most urbane friends to dazzle Callias with their wit. He had also hired a beautiful flautist to entertain his guests together with a female acrobat and, to play the lyre, a boy whose beauty was the current talk of Athens.

Any notions of one-upmanship were banished, however, by the pleasure of seeing Callias. When the last guest had arrived in the courtyard, Charmides gestured to his friend to proceed with him to the doorway of the dining room. Here, each of the guests removed his shoes and had his feet washed by an attendant slave. Charmides directed Callias to the place of honour on the couch next to his own. The slaves arrived with bowls of water in which the company washed their hands, placed a three-legged table in front of each guest and brought round a cup of wine infused with herbs from which everyone sipped in turn. The first course of iris bulbs dressed in vinegar had been well prepared. By contrast, the tuna fish, which should have taken prime place among the fish dishes that followed, was overcooked.

After they had eaten, the slaves cleared the tables away and offered perfume to the guests. The libations to the gods, in which Dionysus, the god of wine, was honoured with a fine vintage from Lesbos, were performed with dignity. Afterwards, each man raised his voice in a hymn to Dionysus. Then Callias won the throw of the dice electing him Lord of the Feast. After each guest had been toasted, Callias ruled that the wine be diluted to allow intelligent conversation. He also proposed that each man should give a dissertation on the nature of goodness.

The entertainers introduced a more ribald note and after they had done their turns everyone relaxed with more wine. Nibbling on titbits (including dried fruit and toasted chickpeas) which the two girls handed around, Charmides could not remember when he had laughed so much especially when the most inebriated of his guests was ordered by Callias, as Lord of the Feast, to carry the flute girl three times around the room as a forfeit for spilling his wine. Even when the last guest smashed a prized cup while levering himself up to go home, he could not help giggling at the sight of the same guest half carried and half dragged from the room by the flute girl who must have been a fraction of his size.

DINING IN STYLE Diners recline at table in a wall painting from the Greek-founded city of Paestum in Italy.

TABLEWARE A fish plate from the 4th century BC is adorned with a cuttlefish, a perch and a torpedo fish.

Generally the Greeks associated eating expensive fish with luxury and eating meat with celebrating the gods.

Also in the 5th century BC women who had previously done all the cooking themselves ceded place to chefs and pastry cooks in a few very rich households. Professional cooks, who came with teams of assistants, competed for the patronage of the rich in much the same way that restaurant chefs do today. They also became a butt of the comic dramatists, who pictured them conducting military-style operations from the kitchen in ludicrous contrast to the peace of the symposia dinners they were cooking for. In ridiculing the over-elaborate presentation of food and its rich ingredients, the dramatists were playing on the disapproval most ordinary people felt for extravagant living of any sort.

Examples of the fare prepared for the rich might include a dish of small fry garnished with sea anemones and the tips of young nettles. Like many

20th-century chefs a new breed of expert, such as Archestratus, emphasised the importance of cooking with fresh, seasonal ingredients. He was contemptuous of vegetables, probably regarding them as poor man's fare, but had a higher opinion of a herb called silphium from the fennel family. Silphium was imported from North Africa and two juices were extracted from the stem and the root. It was a coveted addition to Greek haute cuisine.

THE JOYS OF WINE

The most common drink was water, which the Greeks sometimes sweetened with honey. They also drank goat's milk, and both rich and poor consumed wine. This was fermented in random fashion in vats smeared inside and out with resin. Because there was always a danger of it going off, salt water was added to the wine as a preservative. Compounds of herbs and spices disguised wine that had rotted before reaching its destination. One recorded method of winemaking used liquefied resin mixed with vine ash which was added to the grapes before fermentation.

Typically, Greek wine had a tang to it which was particularly strong in wines intended for home consumption. These might have been fermented for only 24 hours and matured for a week. House wines were stored in pig or goatskin flagons, while those for export were contained in large baked-clay jars, whose insides were painted with pitch. The wine-maker's name and that of the city-state's export controllers were inscribed on the handles.

Although the Greeks showed less interest in different kinds of grapes than the Romans, wines from the islands of Lesbos, Chios and Thasos were considered luxury imports and inspired some lyrical praise. 'You must drink an old wine with a really grey old head,' Archestratus encourages his hedonistic readers; 'its moist locks [are] festooned with white flowers, [it is] born in Lesbos with the sea all around . . . Thasos also produces a noble wine to drink, provided it is aged over many good seasons down the years.' These great vintages were glutinous and sweet – rather like modern fortified wines – and might be matured for as long as 25 years.

ONE FOR THE POT Hares like this one decorating a perfume bottle were usually roasted.

The Greeks drank their wine diluted – the customary strength was two parts wine to five parts water. The water was drawn from the outside well and stored in jars (called *hydrias*) with handles so that they could be lifted onto the heads of women or slaves. The mixing bowl (*crater*) was a large vessel with a wide mouth to allow the mixed wine to be withdrawn in ladles or jugs (*oenochae*) before being poured into cups.

At symposia dinner parties, it was slaves who served the guests, never the women of

KITCHEN TOOLS These bronze utensils include a pot handle (shaped like a double-winged goddess), a bucket-like vessel (or *situla*), a strainer and a bowl. The situla would have been used to store oil or wine.

the household who were not usually allowed into the room. Alternatively, one of the host's sons, if he was too young to recline with the guests himself, might help to serve the wine. This the diners drank from wide, shallow cups (*cylix*) with a stem and a foot. In most households the cups were made of pottery but the very rich had cups fashioned from bronze or silver. Drinking from some of these was made easier by having a portion of the rim raised to help to funnel the liquid into the mouth. Both kinds of cups had sturdy handles which could be used to propel dregs of wine onto a target – a popular symposiac game called *kottabos*. Other games included trying to sink small saucers floating in a bowl.

EYEWITNESS

THE ART OF THE CHEF

ALTHOUGH THEY were scorned for their supposed vulgarity, chefs marketed themselves vigorously in ancient Athens. The more famous ones, such as Archestratus, who wrote one of the first cookery books, were proud of their reputations, as the comic poet Dionysius observed in about the 4th century BC:

❝ Anyone can prepare dishes, carve, boil up sauces and blow on the fire . . . But the chef is something else. To understand the place, the season, the man giving the meal, the guests, when and what fish to buy – that is not a job for just anyone. You will get the same kind of thing just about all the time, but you will not get the same perfection in the dishes or the same flavour [unless you use a chef]. ❞

CLOTHES AND CLEANLINESS

The ancient Greeks took good care of their appearance. Athenian males availed themselves

of bathhouses; women had a range of cosmetics to choose from. Garments were

simple tunics, draped decoratively over the body with the help of pins and girdles.

FROM THE late 5th century onwards, very rich households had bathrooms, usually connected to the kitchen by a pipe that brought in warm air. A slave used a round clay jar to draw water from the well outside. Then he heated it in the kitchen on the way and emptied it into a terracotta bath. This looked very much like a Victorian hipbath and was emptied through a drain pipe issuing outside.

Less wealthy people, meanwhile, would wash themselves at a high-standing basin (*louterion*) on a pedestal, looking rather like a huge brandy glass. This would be fashioned either from elaborately sculpted stone or, more plainly, from terracotta. Basins like these had to be filled from a well and were emptied by hand. The chamber pot, too, was much in use in Greek homes and was emptied into open drains in the street.

Gymnasiums and wrestling schools had fountains, washbasins and even swimming pools, where Greek men could conveniently indulge their social instincts and clean themselves at the same time. The athletes at Delphi had a round pool measuring 10 yd (9 m) in diameter to plunge into after washing themselves down in the basins.

Athens also had bathhouses where men spent hours soaking themselves in hot-water baths that were arranged around a circular room. These were favourite resorts for men on their way home for dinner, having also perhaps stopped in a barber's. Often, the bathhouses had a sauna as well, so that the men could sweat themselves clean before their immersion. Central heating was provided by furnaces manned by slave attendants. Another of the slaves' duties was to rub down the customers and later work oil into their skins. Entrance to a bathhouse was cheap and therefore popular with all sectors of society. Several had a special section for prostitutes, courtesans and slave women.

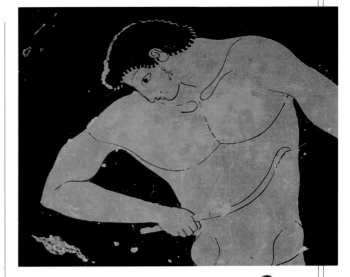

SQUEAKY CLEAN **Having rubbed himself with oil, an athlete scrapes his skin clean using a *strigil* like this bronze one (right).**

In contrast to the Athenians, the Spartans forbade warm baths as unmanly, keeping to icy dips in the River Eurotas instead. Even in Athens, conservatives like the general Demosthenes in the 4th century BC bewailed the habit of visiting the hot baths because 'they make a man slack and effeminate'.

The Greeks used oil rather than soap to clean themselves, working it into the grime that had collected on their bodies and then scraping it off with a *strigil* – a curved metal instrument. Sometimes, they used wood ash or a special kind of clay to much the same astringent effect as we get from mudpacks. There were several night creams on the market for Athenian women.

Oils were also used in beauty aids, for massages and for healing purposes. A superior oil could be obtained from the unripe fruit of olives, sesame, almonds, palms and other plants. Their juice was

A DAY IN THE LIFE OF

A COURTESAN PREPARING FOR THE NIGHT

THE NEW SLAVE girl had not made a good start. Not only had she overheated the water for the washbasin, so that Lysikles' skin had turned an unbecoming red, but she had also applied so much violet perfume to her mistress's neck that it completely masked the myrtle scent on the backs of her knees. Now she was using jugs to empty the basin and in the process slopping the dirty water all over the floor.

But Lysikles' irritation abated when she held up her hand mirror and saw the beautiful chignon the girl had created on the back of her head. Every hair was drawn back from her forehead and the nape of her neck to form a dark mass caught securely in a net. Lysikles opened the lid of the cosmetics container to expose the tops of tall ointment jars and smaller pots of make-up. To have a girl able to dress her hair like that, she reflected, was worth a little scalding.

PERSONAL HYGIENE **A girl washes herself at a *louterion* (hand basin).**

She applied the lead foundation to her face, examining herself critically as she did so. Her naturally dark complexion, she noted, was compensated for by beautiful eyebrows which met, just as they should do, above her nose. She had no need of the false brows that she knew some of her fairer-skinned colleagues hid away in boxes.

Taking up a pot with the inscription 'Lysikles is fair' inscribed on it, she pulled off the tightly fitting lid to reveal the greenish substance inside. First, she carefully applied two perfect circles to her cheekbones before filling in her lips with a lavish amount of the seaweed-based cream. Then she shaded her eyelids with a reddish-brown cream, highlighting the bone above with a jade green one.

She used the same shade of green to draw a line above each eye, meticulously extending the line at both corners. She found the black kohl or lampblack that some of the other girls applied liberally around their eyes had an annoying tendency to smudge by the end of the evening. Nevertheless, she melted a kohl stick of her own over the lamp flame and used it discreetly to blacken her eyelashes and brows.

She was ready to go.

---

extracted and preserved with salt, gum, resin and sometimes honey, vinegar and fennel. An inferior product could be obtained by boiling up wool to produce what we now call lanolin, but the extract tended to rot and produce a terrible smell. Other animal fats, goose fat and butter in particular, were also used in cosmetics.

WELL-TRIMMED HAIR

Athenian men took pride in a well-groomed head of hair. The fashion after the Persian wars was to wear it fairly short, in the Persian style, often with a full beard trimmed to a point or into a spade shape. Only dandies and children wore their hair long, in contrast to the Spartans who shaved their boys and

then permitted long locks for adults. Athenians used perfume on their hair as well as the rest of their bodies.

Razors were principally used by women to rid themselves of body hair. Women never cut their hair, except to honour the dead. Normally, they teased, frizzed and curled their long locks into a mass that they lifted onto the tops of their heads or wore at the napes of their necks in a variety of different fashions. Slave girls had

CLEANSING OIL **Pots like this carried oil, which was used instead of soap.**

excavated from the Athenian Agora, is a double comb made of olive wood, with 31 fine teeth on one side and 20 thicker ones on the other.

By the 4th century BC, many aristocratic women in Athens were using make-up. Rouge, which was slightly thicker than modern cold cream, was sometimes made of vermilion but more often based on vegetable compounds using ingredients as varied as mulberry and seaweed. Many of the products were, in fact, poisonous, and doctors warned of the dire effects of mercury-based creams that caused premature ageing. Lipstick and eye shadow were both used and came in containers with a variety of forms – tripod-style, lidded, open, with a handle and without. They were usually made of clay; some were elaborately decorated.

Unlike their wealthier counterparts, lower-class Athenian women did not paint their faces. In Sparta there was a law that prohibited its citizens from using beauty aids. The Spartan authorities even forbade outsiders who 'used the art of painting the body' from entering the city, on the grounds that such 'evil arts corrupted men's manners'.

WOMEN'S FLOWING ROBES

Women did their best to dress elegantly with relatively simple materials. Their robes were simple rectangles made to a standard length and were folded and pinned together, leaving holes for the head and arms. They girdled the robe so that it fell in flowing folds and pouches. The girdle kept the arrangement of pleats in place and made sure that the woman's right leg was not immodestly displayed while she walked. It also emphasised her upper body to achieve the graceful, dignified look we know from Greek statuary.

A woman could arrange her robe to make a cowl to draw up over her head (appropriate dress for a funeral) or manipulate the material into a double fold at the front which she could use to cover her hands. Alternatively, she might divide the fold in two with her belt.

In the later 5th century BC, some women gave up the pinned woollen garment (*peplos*) in favour

CHANGING STYLES   The heavy plaits of this 6th-century BC woman had fallen out of fashion a century later. For men, trim beards became popular after the Persian wars.

to wear their hair cropped (as did their male counterparts), although slave prostitutes ignored this custom. Little girls commonly wore their hair drawn up into a ponytail on the top of the head or simply pulled back off their faces with a ribbon.

Combs might be made of bone, ivory, bronze or tortoiseshell, according to the owner's wealth. One,

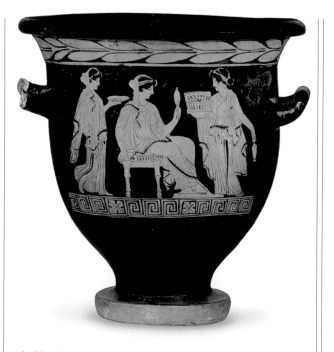

BLOND BEAUTIES

Blond hair was prized by both men and women. 'The sun's rays,' wrote the playwright Menander, 'are the best means for lightening hair, as our men well know. After washing their hair with a special ointment . . . they sit bareheaded in the sun by the hour waiting for their hair to turn a beautiful golden blond.' Failing this, wigs and hair-pieces were used to achieve the same effect.

of a sewn linen tunic. Like the earlier woollen robe, the new tunic (*chiton*) could have a double fold at front and back. In winter, women might supplement this less warm dress with a shawl worn like a sash.

Cloaks, called *himations,* usually reached to the knee or a little below. They consisted of plain oblongs with decorated edges that women inge-niously pinched, pleated and arranged in a variety of different fashions. The folds might fall in the front rather than behind, or a woman could fold the length into several thicknesses and drape it over the back of her arms to form a stole.

While most Greek men and women wore similar clothing, young Spartan girls were an exception. The small pieces of material they had to cover themselves with provoked many ribald comments from the Athenians. Their short open dresses,

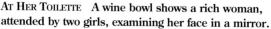

AT HER TOILETTE   A wine bowl shows a rich woman, attended by two girls, examining her face in a mirror.

which doubled up as tunics and cloaks, consisted of a thin length of woollen material attached at the shoulders and worn without a girdle. Plutarch described 'these quasi-tunics, the skirt of which, not being sewn from the hem, fell open as the wearer walked, revealing her thighs; whence the nickname they were given, "thigh-displayers".'

SCENT CONTAINERS   Perfume bottles came in many forms, shaped like animals, even like sandalled feet. The fashion for perfume reached Greece from Egypt.

FEMALE GARB
The *peplos* (left) was fastened at the shoulders with long pins. Athenian women started to wear the *chiton* (below) – tied to give them longer, fuller sleeves – around the mid 6th century BC.

For most Greek women the materials available to them were wool and plain linen which might be striped and were sometimes fringed – favourite colours were saffron and red. The wealthy had a greater choice that included finely crinkled linen, with a texture like that of crepe, and sometimes muslin. The fine flax that grew on the island of Amorgos was particularly sought after; it was worked into richly embroidered linen tunics for export. Lengths of silk from Cos were also coveted. Dresses made from Cos silk clung to the flesh diaphanously, prompting the writer Theocritus in the 3rd century BC to call them 'wet garments'. The long linen robes produced in Corinth were another item desired by the fashionable, while nearby Pellene in Achaea in the northern Peloponnese did a brisk trade in mantles.

The Athenian housewife, like her husband, wore no underwear beneath her tunic, beyond a slip or a broad belt to elevate the breasts. Prostitutes might use a stomach bandage to hide unsightly bulges or disguise an unwanted pregnancy. They might also add to their height with cork soles in their slippers and increase the breadth of scanty hips with well-placed padding. The more respectable housewife, however, was expected to live a life of secluded industriousness within the home, and had mostly to be content with the figure the gods gave her.

ORIENTAL LUXURY, SPARTAN SIMPLICITY

The Greeks were both attracted and repelled by the oriental luxury they had seen while they were battling with the Persians in the 5th century BC. On the one hand, commentators complained that their countrymen were emulating foppish eastern ways by such habits as wearing purple cloaks, going about dripping with perfume and paying too much attention to their hair.

On the other hand, the defeat of the Persians brought about a reaction against the luxurious

HAIR STYLING Women plaited their hair or wore it up, using a net or ribbon to hold it in place. Only slaves or women in mourning cut it short.

habits of the Greeks' enemies. This was noticeable among the Athenians, in particular, who started to emulate the simplicity of Spartan dress. As Thucydides noted, they gave up their habit of 'going about their daily life fully armed and doing their hair up in buns fastened with golden grasshoppers'.

By the 5th century BC, male costume for the poor and slaves and some wealthier men had been abbreviated to a plain tunic made of woven wool or flax (usually imported from Ionia) or a coarse material spun from goats' hair. These tunics, like women's robes, were rectangles, often with one or two sewn seams, which men draped loosely around themselves and secured at the shoulders with a knot or pin. The pins were originally made from the leg bones of small animals but were later fashioned from metal. The tunic was pinched in at the waist with a girdle, beneath which it hung down in folds. Occasionally, men wore another belt higher up to make a second tier of folds. At night, they removed the girdle in order to turn the tunic into a nightshirt – they had spare tunics, of course, and changed them regularly so that the dirty ones could be washed. Despite the newer fashion for short tunics, the longer ones that had been worn in the 6th century BC were still seen on ceremonial occasions, notably on priests and minstrels.

Men's *himations* (cloaks) were oblongs of woollen material. They were either plain for everyday use or made from fine wool, often with coloured stripes woven into them, for more special occasions. The himation was fastened over one shoulder, leaving the other shoulder and the chest naked. To wear a himation too far below the knee was considered a sign of arrogant extravagance – Alcibiades in his youth often gave offence by doing this. Equally, to wear it above the knee was considered indecent, and to sit down so that the garment rose up above the knee was simply wanton. Despite such prejudices, many Athenian dandies affected elaborate himations which they sported along with a tall stick with a forked head. They leant on the stick when they stood still, so that the fold of the cloak was held in place under the armpit.

There was an art to putting on himations, known as 'dressing to the right'. The wearer first spread the cloak over his shoulders and back, letting two corners hang down in front of him. Then he stretched out his right arm to gather up the two hanging folds, and drew them across his left arm or else draped them over his left shoulder so that they fell in a point. He next took up the fold of the cloak in his right hand and brought it across to the right, before finally passing it back over the left shoulder. One's dexterity in dressing to the right was a mark of breeding, while getting things the wrong way round – that is, dressing to the left – was the mark

EYEWITNESS
A LIFE OF LUXURY

THE COMIC PLAYWRIGHT Antiphanes of the early 4th century BC describes a dilettante youth, who bathes:

❝ . . . in gilded tub and steeps his feet
And legs in rich Egyptian unguents;

His neck and chest he rubs with oil of palm,
And both his arms with sweet extract of mint,
His eyebrows and his hair with marjoram,
His knees and face with essence of wild thyme. ❞

SUN SHADE Travellers and huntsmen wore broad-brimmed hats to protect them from the sun.

of a barbarian (or foreigner). Socrates, according to Plato, was contemptuous of country bumpkins 'who do not know how to fold their himation over the left shoulder like freeborn citizens'.

To give themselves greater freedom for manoeuvre, soldiers sometimes folded their cloaks lengthwise and pinned them to their left shoulders. Alternatively, they wore thicker, shorter cloaks called *chlamys* that were designed particularly for warfare. These were pinned at the shoulder to allow greater manoeuvrability. The chlamys' drawbacks were that they tended to balloon out behind the runner or rider and could impede the arm on the side on which they were fastened.

BRACELETS, ANKLETS AND SANDALS

By the 5th century BC, men wore signet rings, but otherwise they had abandoned such adornments as the grasshopper brooches sported by the warriors who fought in the Persian wars.

Women, by contrast, wore an abundance of jewellery including necklaces, which sometimes had amulets hanging from them, and bands of gold or silver with ornamental clasps on their wrists and upper arms. Sometimes, the bracelets took the form of a snake curled around itself and were very beautiful indeed. Anklets were another common ornament worn on a day-to-day basis. Women also wore small circular studs in their pierced ears.

These might be patterned or they might have an amulet hanging from them. All of these precious things were kept in jewellery caskets brought to a rich woman by her slave when a public festival gave her an opportunity to dress up.

Rich women had parasols to protect their complexions from the hot sun. These were constructed like modern umbrellas with a piece of circular material stretched over ribs that could be opened and closed by means of a sliding ring over the handle. Expensive models had spikes protruding beyond the edge of the material. They could also be used as protection from rain and were held above the mistress by her personal slave who walked behind her.

Both men and women usually went barefoot within the house, but wore ankle boots of felt or leather outside. For their footwear, men went to the cobbler who cut out the soles around their feet. Sandals consisted of a plain sole of cork, wood or leather attached to the leg by leather thongs and a loop for the big toe: such sandals have periodically been in fashion ever since. Ankle boots, laced up the front and sometimes with turnovers were worn by male travellers, but were commonly regarded as feminine apparel. There were more varieties of women's shoes, which were usually dyed black, red, white or yellow. The towns of Argos, Sicyon and Rhodes were especially renowned for their delicate footwear.

Men wore wide-brimmed hats when they were travelling, and peasants and lower-class city-dwellers sometimes wore plain felt or woollen bonnets – as did, according to legend, Hephaestus, the god of metalworkers. No Athenian male with any degree of social standing, however, would be seen in such a hat. Women might wear a cap or a veil or a narrow 'sweatband'. They might also wear a headscarf or a round, wide-brimmed hat with a pointed crown.

GETTING DRESSED
A woman sits naked on a cushion as she pulls on her sandals. A scarf keeps her hair in place.

THE GREEKS AT WORK

Everyone worked in ancient Greece, and some worked very hard indeed.

From the peasant trying to supplement the family diet by trapping

birds (above) to the craftsman working alongside his assistants,

countryman and city-dweller alike laboured from dawn to dusk.

Even rich men who employed slave labour to work their

estates kept themselves busy with civic and political duties.

POWER IN ACTION

The old aristocratic leaders of the Greek states accepted democracy with bad grace,

grumbling about the newly rich political and military leaders who had come to the fore.

In the democracies, every citizen could be called upon to serve the state in public office.

THE CORINTHIAN statesman Sosicles was a stout defender of democracy. In the last decade of the 6th century BC the Spartans were worried by an increasingly democratic and powerful Athens and proposed intervention by other Greek states to restore its former tyrant Hippias. Sosicles, however, gave them short shrift. 'Upon my word, gentlemen,' he expostulated in an account by the historian Herodotus, 'this is like turning the universe upside-down. Earth and sky will soon be changing places – men will be living in the sea and fish on land, now that you Spartans are proposing to abolish democratic government and restore despotism in the cities. Believe me, there is nothing wickeder or bloodier in the world than despotism.'

In the event, Hippias remained in exile and the democratic wave gained momentum across the Greek world during the 5th century. Ordinary people in many city-states won increasing power, and

IRRIGATING STREAM **The Eurotas river meanders across the plain of Sparta.**

although a noble name continued to elicit respect, the old aristocratic families lost much of their former influence. In the old days, prowess as a warrior leader had been the surest path to political success. Now, ordinary men took to the political arena as demagogues (professional public speakers). One was Cleon, a successful tanner, who became Athens' dominant politician after the great democratic statesman Pericles died in 429.

PAYMENT FOR OFFICE

Athens in the age of Pericles and Cleon was the supreme example of democracy in action, with power spread across a large cross-section of the citizen body – the largest in Greece, though it never exceeded 50 000 people, excluding as it did women, slaves and resident foreigners (*metics*). An Athenian citizen needed only to be 30 or over and have a good reputation to be eligible for a wide selection of offices. In Athens, unlike other states, an official was also paid a modest daily wage in order to encourage him to devote himself to his administrative duties.

MIGHT IS RIGHT Sparta's influence depended on men like this – the most formidable warriors in the Greek-speaking world.

Most citizens could expect to hold office at some time in their lives – although Athenian officials, unlike those in modern democracies, were selected by lot rather than being elected. Tenure was usually for a year, and they were accountable to their fellow citizens through regular checks. The civil year was divided into ten 'months' and in each there was an opportunity for the Assembly of the People, composed of all citizens, to vote on whether current officials should stay in place. At the end of the year the magistrates had to undergo an audit (*euthyna*) by the Council, or Boule, the executive arm of the Assembly. The Council scrutinised their con-

FLATTERY AND FIGS

Sycophants – those who try to win power for themselves by flattering people of influence – originated in classical Athens. In those days, they were men who made their living by blackmailing the rich with threats to bring a public case against them. Literally, the word meant 'fig-shower'. It may have had an obscene significance, although another possible explanation is that the word was originally connected with protests against the illegal export of figs.

duct and bookkeeping over the year, and anyone found wanting went before the law courts.

Serving on the Council was the most important of all the posts to which a citizen could be delegated. It consisted of 500 men who were drawn in equal proportions from the ten different 'tribes' that made up the Athenian population. Each tribal group took its turn to serve as the Prytaneis, or executive committee, for one of the ten 'months' of the civil year. The 50 men lived and ate at state expense in the Round House (*Prytaneum*). The chairman was selected daily by lot and could serve only once; he chaired the Assembly if it met on his day. Potter or aristocrat, everyone in the Council had a 70 per cent chance of chairing it for a day.

The Council had a wide range of responsibilities including preparing business for the Assembly to discuss and ensuring that the Assembly's decisions

THE MERITS OF DEMOCRACY

PEOPLE POWER Democracy crowns Demos, the people of Athens. Inscribed below is a law designed to protect Athenian democracy.

WHICH was best – democracy (rule by all), oligarchy (rule by a few) or monarchy (rule by one)? All three were practised in different Greek states and each had its advocates. The 5th-century BC historian Herodotus reports a discussion of their merits which he puts into the mouths of three Persian nobles.

The first speaker, a democrat, has no truck with monarchy which, in his opinion, encourages *hubris* (pride) and excess in the ruler:

❛ How can it admit of proper adjustment when it allows one man to do what he likes without being answerable for it? Even the best of men put in that position is bound to overstep the bounds of normality. The advantages he enjoys breed pride, and envy is deeply engrained in human nature. A man with these two faults is wholly evil . . . The worst feature of all is that he breaks down traditional law and custom, puts men to death without trial and subjects women to sexual violence. The rule of the people on the other hand has the most attractive of descriptions, rule by all . . . Offices are filled by lot, officials are answerable for what they do, and all questions are publicly debated.'

The second speaker is an oligarch who agrees with the first in his mistrust of rule by one person, but is equally afraid of the opposite extreme, rule by the 'mob':

'To be rid of the violence of a tyrant only to fall under the violence of an uncontrollable mob would be intolerable. A tyrant at least knows what he is doing, the people has no knowledge at all. How can it have, being uneducated and without sense of what is right and proper? It rushes mindlessly into public affairs like a river in flood.'

The last speaker, by contrast, is a monarchist who supports the current Persian king:

'There can be nothing better than government by the best man. With his abilities his control of the people will be above criticism, and the measures he takes against wrongdoers will have maximum secrecy . . . I ask where did we get our present freedom from and who gave it to us? My view is that as we were given our freedom by one man we should preserve that kind of constitution; and quite apart from this, it is never an improvement to change ancestral laws and customs so long as they work well. ❜

laws as well as general policy. Emergency assemblies could be called at any time by the generals, the most important of all officials who, unlike most others, were elected rather than being chosen by lot. In 346 BC when Alexander the Great's father, Philip of Macedon, had captured the central Greek state of Elateia, bringing him dangerously close to Athenian territory, the councillors advertised a crisis meeting by setting fire to the traders' stalls in the market.

The first meeting of each of the ten 'months' of the civil year was known as the 'sovereign meeting', and this was when the grain supply, national defence and the continuation in office of the state officials was debated. If anyone wished to bring an impeachment against another citizen this, too, was the day to do it.

Purification rites started proceedings, followed by a ritual cursing of all traitors. Then a herald read out the agenda and the people voted on whether or not they wished to discuss the listed issues.

DANGEROUS VOCATION Even the statesman Pericles (above) was once threatened with ostracism – ten years banishment from Athens – as is shown by his name scratched on a pottery voting shard (right).

were carried out. Various subcommittees and boards supervised the levying of fines and the executing of other financial transactions.

It seems surprising that this government of amateurs worked so well, but councillors did receive backup. Trained slaves acting as clerks were probably available, and every kind of transaction was written down so that new councillors could refer to precedents. There were also endless checks and counterchecks in the form of audits and appeals to the law courts to prevent corruption. Most people, too, had experience of serving on their village (or deme) councils. Even so, the fisherman or craftsman who found himself in a position of power must have depended as much on his common sense as on previous experience to carry out his tasks.

THE PEOPLE'S ASSEMBLY

The full Assembly, which included the whole citizen body, sat 40 times a year. Its members congregated on the Pnyx hill west of the Acropolis and voted on

After that the herald asked 'Who wishes to speak?' Each speaker, after being announced by the herald, placed a myrtle wreath around his head to mark himself out as the speaker and mounted a stone platform. This was situated with the audience ranked in a semicircle above and around it. The council committee sat on one side of the speaker and a police force of slaves maintained order. In theory, it was possible for anyone to hold forth; in practice, the man in the street was likely to be shouted down by his equals in favour of a skilled rhetorician who could marshal

---

DRACONIAN MEASURES

The word *draconian* derives from the legendarily harsh series of laws attributed to the 7th-century BC Athenian legislator Dracon. They included the death penalty for the majority of criminal offences. Solon repealed them for a more lenient code in the 6th century BC.

EYEWITNESS

BARROW-BOY STATESMANSHIP

THE PLAYWRIGHT Aristophanes (*c*.448-*c*.387 BC) was no lover of demagogues. He attacked them disdainfully in remarks to a sausage-maker who wanted to know the secret of political influence:

❛ There's nothing to it; just carry on in your usual way. Mangle and make mincemeat of everything, and win over the *demos* [that is, the people] by always sweetening them with your cook-shop rhetoric. You've got all the other qualifications for a leader of the demos, a filthy voice, common birth and barrow-boy character – yes, everything you need for statesmanship. ❜

all the relevant information and impress the mass meeting. The atmosphere could get extremely excitable as the competitive, loquacious Athenians debated issues such as the corn supply or defence.

Individual politicians thrived on the envy their pre-eminence inspired and boasted of their achievements and public services to secure the people's ear. It was a glorious but precarious career to pursue. The pecuniary rewards for successful politicians were meagre, and they risked prosecution for misleading the crowd. In the 5th and 4th centuries, most of the leading lights in the political arena were subjected to some sort of trial which usually ended in a heavy fine, exile or even execution.

Even the generals, who could conduct war without informing the Assembly about strategic detail, risked being taken to court. And in any field, a reputation for talent or brilliance was not necessarily a

TALKING POLITICS With a myrtle wreath around his head, a speaker holds forth to the Athenian Assembly. It met on the Pnyx hill, a rocky outcrop west of the city.

recommendation. According to the historian Thucydides, the conservative politician Antiphon 'had a most powerful intellect' as well as natural oratorical gifts, but even in his prime he 'never came forward to speak in front of the Assembly unless he could help it . . . or competed in any other form of public life, since the people in general mistrusted him because of his reputation for cleverness'.

JUSTICE FOR ALL

Equality before the law was one of the boldest and most novel features of Greek, particularly Athenian, democracy. Because the Athenians were an intensely litigious people, there were many courts scattered across their city. Murder cases, for instance, were tried in a designated open-air space to avoid contamination from the pollution of death. Athens had 40 circuit judges who travelled through the demes (villages) to try cases where the penalty, if

IT'S A LOTTERY
The Athenians chose most officials by lot – using pottery tokens like these – rather than electing them.

the defendant was found guilty, was assessed at below 10 drachma. Cases involving potentially higher fines were tried by judges aged over 60.

Every year 6000 citizens – 600 from each tribe – went onto a list that acted as a pool from which

jurymen were selected at random. Courts were not generally specialised – they tried any case that came before them. The number of jurors could vary from 201 to 2501 depending on the importance of the case; the administrators always insisted on an odd number to prevent a split vote. Pericles first instituted payment for jury service at 2 obols a day. This was increased by Cleon to 3 obols. Although it was less than an average labourer could earn in a day, conservatives complained that the juries were filled with ignorant poor people out for an easy day's wage. For the democrats, the advantage of this system was that it encouraged even poor people to miss work for a day to serve as jurymen and thus play their part in safeguarding democracy.

Elaborate precautions were taken to preserve the anonymity of the jurors and so prevent bribery. On the day of the hearing, the juror would rise at dawn and make his way through the darkened streets to a court. Here, he registered with a magistrate at the doorway designated for each tribe. Each man carried an identity

WATER TIME Water clocks measured the time during which each litigant in a court case could speak.

badge made of wood or stone with his name inscribed on it. He posted the badge into an allotment machine which randomly selected jurors and allocated them to a court. The complicated rigmarole worked like a multiple lottery. In the court the jury was fenced off from spectators who gathered in the entrance way. Once the court was in session the doors were closed.

Court cases could be noisy and melodramatic affairs. Although the jury's function was solely to listen, they often made their sympathies evident by 'murmuring', which evidently could become a roar. According to Plato, Socrates had to plead with the jury not to shout him down when he was presenting his defence against a capital charge in 399 BC.

In the absence of a public prosecutor, the Greeks brought their own cases for trial. Family quarrels were customarily settled out of court with the help of relations who would act as arbitrators. If a settlement was not reached in this way, the aggrieved party might choose to go to court. Each case (however complicated) was allowed a maximum of one day's hearing and the jury voted without any direction from a judge or any time to consider the issues out of court. There was no cross-examination of witnesses or rules about evidence. Nor were there lawyers to represent the litigants. The accused and the accuser simply battled it out in turn, flattering and cajoling the jurors and trying to convince them that they were modest fellows, men of the people, natural enemies of wealth and power. Litigants sometimes turned to professional speechwriters who wrote their speeches for them.

THE JOYS OF THE JUROR BUSINESS

IN HIS PLAY *The Wasps*, Aristophanes satirised the Athenians fondness for litigation – the plot involves the mock trial of a dog charged with stealing a cheese. He also poked fun at the supposed mania among the elderly for jury service. Here he depicts one such enthusiast:

❝ He loves it, this juror business; and he groans if he can't sit on the front bench. He doesn't get a wink of sleep at night, but if in fact he does doze off just for a moment, his mind still flies through the night to the water clock . . . Straight after supper he shouts for

his shoes, and then off he goes to the court in the early hours and sleeps there, clinging to the column like a limpet. And through bad temper he awards the long line [heaviest penalty] to all the defendants, and then comes home like a bee. ❞

GUILTY OR NOT GUILTY Jurors queue to drop their tokens into two urns: one for acquittal, the other for conviction. A magistrate and two court officials watch from the dais.

A water clock determined the time during which each litigant could present his case. The length of time depended on the size of the penalty. The clock was stopped during the reading of documents or calling of witnesses. The litigant explained the law to the jury and interpreted it to benefit his case. His adversary did the same. Both parties might boast of their public generosity and good social standing to influence the jury. Poorer men might produce snivelling children (sometimes borrowed) and work on the jury's feelings with elaborate 'sob stories'.

When both sides had presented their cases, the jurors filed past two urns – one for acquittal and one for conviction – each juror placing a pebble or shell in the appropriate urn. To prepare themselves, some jurors might have read Solon's law code displayed on great wooden beams in the market, but most would have found the code's convoluted language inaccessible. Instead a juryman relied on his common sense, humanity and previous experience to direct his vote after the speeches.

Later, special balloting devices were used. A disc with a hollow centre was for a vote for the prosecution; one with a solid centre was for the

defence. Each juror had one of each, and dropped the one that corresponded with his vote in one urn, and the other into a discard bin.

Penalties ranged from imprisonment or a fine to exile, with the confiscation of one's property and civilian rights, or death. If the fine was beyond a citizen's means, he could avoid it by going into voluntary exile. Citizens were treated differently from slaves, who could be whipped on a wheel, branded with red-hot irons or sentenced to the stocks.

A very cruel form of execution was known as pegging out. The victim was taken outside the city walls, stripped and his limbs and neck fixed by metal clamps to a stake or wall. Here he remained until he died, the metal collar biting into his jaw as he hung upright. Pericles imposed this death on rebels from the island of Samos, part of the Athenian Empire, who after ten days' hanging were taken down and clubbed to death. In comparison, Socrates was permitted a relatively humane method of execution when he was allowed to swallow hemlock.

SECRET BALLOT Discs with spindles (left) for not guilty and ones with a hole (far left) for guilty were introduced in the 4th century BC.

IN THE ARMY AND NAVY

A Greek male's economic circumstances determined whether

he fought for his state as a cavalry officer or foot soldier or,

in Athens, was recruited for the navy.

MANY ABLE-BODIED Greek men went to war almost every year of their lives, not for territorial reasons, but to assert their states' political dominance over others. Truces were made for limited periods only. The longest was the 30 year peace drawn up by Sparta and Athens in 446 BC, in which Sparta effectively acknowledged Athens as Greece's greatest sea power, while Athens acknowledged Sparta's supremacy on land. In the event, this lasted only 15 years. More than a generation of official peace was unthinkable.

In Athens, a citizen was liable for military call-up from the ages of 20 to 60. He would discover his posting from the notice board in the marketplace and would immediately return home to prepare himself for departure. He was paid a small daily sum depending on the state of treasury funds. The Spartan citizen, by contrast, dedicated his entire life from early childhood to warfare. He was a professional who waged war in the same way as other Greeks, but with much more skill and courage.

The Athenians needed to be harangued by their leaders at the beginning of a fight. Spartan warriors, wearing crimson cloaks to hide blood stains and with their long locks combed out, needed no such encouragement. The Spartans marched with slow precision towards their opponents singing martial songs. They usually maintained their formations throughout (other Greek armies tried to do so but in practice often surged forward in disarray), changing with consummate dexterity and speed from marching column to battle alignment before they entered the fray.

HOPLITE FIGHTING

The hoplite (foot soldier) was the mainstay of 5th-century BC Greek armies. He had to be rich enough to provide his own armour and was therefore enlisted from the ranks of the middle class.

On the long, slow journey to enemy territory, the fear of death would not probably have been at the forefront of the hoplite's mind, since there were comparatively few fatalities during Greek wars. According to the historian Herodotus, just 91 Spartans, 16 Tegeans and 52 Athenians, out of a total of some 110 000 Greek soldiers, were killed at the Battle of Plataea against the Persians in 479 BC.

One reason for these low casualty figures was that the hoplite was heavily armoured. His metal helmet was felt-lined and adorned with a crest which followed the curve of the headpiece; hinged cheek-plates protected his face and sometimes he had a visor for the nose. He also wore a breastplate and back plate joined together by hooks or buckles.

CLOSE COMBAT A vase shows two warriors, armed with shields and swords, fighting hand to hand.

COUNCIL OF WAR A 4th-century BC Greek artist working in southern Italy depicted the Persian king Darius (enthroned in the centre) taking advice as he decided whether or not to invade Greece.

The hoplite's principal weapon was a 6 ft (1.8 m) wooden thrusting spear ending in a thin metal arrow or cone. He held it at shoulder level, jabbing it at the gap between his enemy's helmet and breastplate. For face-to-face fighting, he used a 2 ft (61 cm) single-edged sword which he slashed downwards on his enemy. He also had a small dagger. His round shield was made of bronze, and a little less than 3 ft (91 cm) across.

Cavalrymen came from among the rich as only the wealthy could afford to maintain a horse on parched Greek lands. Even at its biggest Athens' cavalry division consisted of only 1000 men. Armed with two throwing spears and a sabre which he had to manipulate as he rode bareback, the cavalryman was easily thrown. Cavalry were principally used to spy out enemy troops, as messengers or to provide diversionary tactics during battle. They

CAVALRY OFFICER
This bronze statuette came from the Spartan colony of Taras (Taranto) in southern Italy.

HARNESSING FLAME POWER

Boeotian soldiers in 424 BC devised a primitive flamethrower. They attached a cauldron to a hollowed-out beam and filled it with lighted coals, sulphur and pitch. They fitted a pair of bellows to the other end of the beam. The blast from the bellows produced a great flame that set light to a fort their Athenian enemies were defending.

were also effective against isolated groups of hoplites or for harassing columns on the move.

Archers, stone-throwers and slingers were drawn from the poorest sector of society. They engaged in preliminary skirmishes with the advancing enemy. They had no protective armour beyond a flimsy shield and a bonnet-shaped helmet. They were effective in rough or hilly country where they could outmanoeuvre more heavily laden hoplites.

RUNNING HOME FROM MARATHON

The army also had foot messengers to deliver news to the civilians at home. The most famous was the Athenian Pheidippides who ran back to his city after the Athenian victory over the Persians at Marathon in 490 BC. The story went that he ran the 26 miles (42 km) without stopping, managed to gasp out the words 'Rejoice, we conquer!' and then dropped dead with exhaustion. Less dramatically, signal fires were used to telegraph news.

EYEWITNESS

STOMPING FROM THE FIELD OF BATTLE

PLATO GIVES an account of the young politician Alcibiades hailing Socrates as the Athenians fled from pursuing Spartans at Delium in 424 BC:

❛ Our troops were in headlong flight; and there was Socrates, stomping along with [another Athenian] Laches. At this point I rode over, the moment I spotted him shouting "Don't lose heart, I'll see you through all right" . . . being mounted, I was in less danger and the first thing that struck me was how much more composed and sensible he was than Laches . . . He was stalking along . . . with the same calm stare for friend and foe alike, but making it very clear . . . that he would give a good account of himself if he was molested. It was this that enabled both him and Laches to get clear away: no one cares to tangle with his sort of character in battle when there are frantic fugitives to be chased. ❜

HEAVY METAL A column of hoplites, bristling with spears, presents a wall of shields to the foe. With them are flute players and cavalrymen.

Preparation for war involved much consultation with oracles. The Athenian general Nicias, a particularly pious man, equipped himself with images of his city's patron gods, together with a portable altar, before setting out on campaign. Then, when two armies were in sight of each other, the gods were consulted again. The Spartans at Plataea in 479 BC remained passive under a storm of Persian arrows because the gods had not responded in time and gave them the authorisation to move into action – despite which the Greeks won the day.

Hoplites moved in lines eight men deep and then closed ranks at the last minute so that their shields overlapped. This presented a wall of metal with which they crashed into their opponents. As each side pushed against the other, it tried to break up the opposing ranks. Once an army was in retreat the cavalry came into play, pursuing the retreating soldiers or harrying the victors to give cover to their own escaping men.

Captured soldiers were usually enslaved or ransomed rather than killed. Each side buried its own dead. Spartan soldiers were buried in their crimson cloaks and covered with olive branches. Athenians cremated their dead in vast funeral pyres and then recovered the bones for return to Athens. Because battle casualties were comparatively few, the worst damage was usually inflicted by 'ravaging' the land. This meant the systematic destruction of enemy crops, olive trees and buildings.

By the 4th century BC, tactics had changed. The shortcomings of the cumbersome hoplite had been shown up during the Peloponnesian War. The hoplite's role had been supplemented by soldiers equipped with wickerwork shields, who were considered more effective in hit-and-run operations.

FIGHTING FIT Among the wild Thracians of northern Greece, even the women were sometimes warriors.

This was an age of the mercenaries when lightly armed troops, such as slingers from Rhodes or bowmen from Crete, were out for hire. Though conservatives like the Athenian orator Demosthenes bewailed the end of a patriotic age, these specialist soldiers were more competent than the citizen soldiers of earlier times.

RULING THE WAVES

Attica's Laurium silver mines, a key source of Athenian wealth, largely financed the Athenian navy of 200 battleships that defeated the Persians at Salamis in 480 BC. Thereafter,

during the 5th century, Athens maintained 300-400 warships financed by the tribute it exacted from its subject states. Beyond this, rich citizens were nominated annually to fit out warships (the state provided the skeleton boat) and maintain them at sea for a year as part of their civic obligations.

Athenian warships (triremes) were long, thin ships with two low-slung banks of portholes for the oars – the third tier poked over the side. The rowers were all paid, the top rank commanding the biggest salary because their oars were at the sharpest angle to the water and therefore the hardest to wield.

At the front was a ramming post or 'beak'.

SYNCHRONISED STROKES A quartermaster sets the rhythm as rowers move in for attack (left). A modern reconstruction of a trireme (below) – officially a vessel of the Greek navy – ploughs through the Aegean.

EYEWITNESS

ARTEMISIA – AMAZON OF THE SEAS

HALICARNASSUS, on the coast of modern Turkey, was the birthplace of the Greek historian Herodotus. At the time of the Battle of Salamis (480 BC), it was part of the Persian Empire. Here, Herodotus describes the part its warrior-queen Artemisia played, on the Persian side:

❛ I cannot offer a precise account of how anyone else fought . . . but as far as Artemisia is concerned, this is what happened, and as a result of it she rose in King Xerxes' estimation. The king's forces had been thrown into great confusion, and . . . Artemisia's ship was being chased by an Athenian ship. She wasn't able to get away (three friendly ships were in her way, and her own ship happened to be closest to the enemy). So she decided to act as follows, and the plan worked out well for her. As she was being pursued by the Athenian ship, she attacked at full speed a friendly ship, manned by Calyndians . . . Whether she had been involved in a dispute with him while they were at the Hellespont, I can't say; nor whether her action was premeditated or whether the Calyndian ship had the bad luck to get in her way. In any case, she attacked it and sank it, and used her good luck to get herself a double advantage. When the captain of the Athenian ship saw that she was attacking a Persian ship, he thought that Artemisia's ship either was Greek or had defected from the Persians . . . so he turned away and took off after other ships. That was the first benefit, to be able to get away and not be killed. The second was that by doing damage she rose higher . . . in Xerxes' estimation. The story goes that when the king . . . saw her ship making its attack, one of the bystanders said: "Master, do you see how well Artemisia is fighting and that she has sunk an enemy ship?" The king asked if this were truly Artemisia's achievement, and they confirmed that it was . . . ; they believed that the ship she had destroyed was the enemy's. In addition . . . she had the good luck that there were no survivors from the Calyndian ship to accuse her. Xerxes is said to have remarked on what he had been told: "My men have turned into women, and my women into men." ❜

There was a mast, yard and square sail, although wind power was used only when well out of sight of the enemy. For battle the mast was left on shore or laid at rest along a crutch, and the rowers took charge. The ship was steered with two large oars fixed on either side of the poop.

The triremes were the fastest ships on the seas. Using both wind and manpower they could reach speeds of 7 to 8 knots (8 to 9 mph – 13 to 15 km/h) or even 13 knots (15 mph – 24 km/h) for short bursts of ten minutes or so. They were each manned by 180 rowers recruited from among the poorest citizens. Aristotle attributed the rise of Athenian democracy to the 'naval throng', members of the poorer classes who found themselves with something of a whip hand in politics. But with a total of 40 000 men needed to power the navy, the rowers were frequently resident foreigners (metics) or mercenaries from outside Athens.

The sailors had to provide their own oars – which could be up to 14 ft (4.2 m) long, depending on which bank of oarsmen they belonged to. The ship's captain was the citizen who had paid for the ship, accompanied by an experienced first lieutenant as steersman or navigator.

The ships were light and fragile, and great skill and training were needed to circumnavigate the treacherous currents which formed around the island-dotted seascape of the Aegean. The principle tactical manoeuvre was to break through enemy lines and swing round, either ramming the enemy ships through the middle or cutting off their oars. Dexterous turns, speed of movement and accuracy of attack were all essential to success. The Athenian sailors, with experience of patrolling their empire, excelled at these skills.

A handful of hoplite soldiers was sometimes included among the sailors to fight off the enemy once two ships were locked together in combat. If their ship was rammed the sailors tried to bail it out and if this failed they broke it up to provide rafters on which they could float ashore.

MAKING A LIVING

The majority of the Greek population were farmers, aspiring to no more than

self-sufficiency from tilling their small arid plots of land. In the cities, craftsmen might run

small workshops or hire themselves out for work on state constructions.

MOST GREEKS LIVED from the land, working the network of smallholdings reached by rough tracks that divided up the countryside. City-dwellers such as the Athenian Xenophon liked to praise the 'manly vigour' derived from the long hours the peasant farmer spent tilling his land. In their opinion, these farmers made the city-state's best fighters because in defending the state they were also defending their produce. They made the best citizens, too, because of the managerial skills they acquired in running a farm. The playwright Aristophanes similarly painted a rosy picture of rural life: 'Remember, gentlemen . . . the figs both fresh and dried, the myrtle and the sweet wine, violets blowing beside the well, the olives we miss so much.' He seems to have had little notion of how hard the farmer's life could actually be.

The reality was definitely harsh. There was a perennial shortage of good agricultural land and the climate was far from propitious. The only way of dealing with heavy rainfall in autumn and winter and drought during the summer was by carefully ploughing the soil three times a year to help it to retain its moisture. Farmers in Attica grew barley but although there was considerable interest in seeds, they could not produce enough grain to support the population. As a result, large quantities had to be imported from other states, notably those along the Black Sea.

Major landlords were able to harvest big crops from their vineyards and olive groves, while figs also gave a good yield. The peasant farmer, however, aspired simply to self-sufficiency – he rarely had a marketable surplus – and supplemented his farming produce with a vegetable garden. Shepherds led lonely lives, herding their flocks of sheep, goats and pigs around the hills in summer and driving them down into the valleys in winter. They never kept many cows which required too much grazing and were rare except as draught animals. Other peasants kept bees or found jobs as charcoal-burners on the wooded slopes of mountains.

WORK OF PLOUGH AND SPADE

Agricultural techniques in the 5th century BC had made little advance on the 8th-century methods described by the curmudgeonly farmer-cum-poet Hesiod, a native of the Boeotian plain west of Attica.

HARDY STOCK Sheep and the olive (opposite) were both able to thrive on the infertile Greek land.

EYEWITNESS

A WORLD FULL OF BEES AND SHEEP AND OLIVES

THE ATHENIAN playwright Aristophanes pictures the contrast between the farming and the city life: ❛ I led the most enjoyable kind of rustic existence, one of the Great Unwashed, never bothered by bugs, lying around any old how, my world full of bees and sheep and olives. And then I went and married a regular city belle . . . and when we got in the bridal bed together, there was I stinking of wine-lees, drying figs and greasy wool-bales, while she was redolent of myrrh and saffron. ❜

A Peasant Farmer in Attica

YOU'VE SEEN the farmhouse – that doesn't take long – and here next door to it is the garden where we grow our fruit trees and vegetables and the place where the pigs and chickens root about. If you look out towards the left you can see my fields. The vineyards are scattered about all over the place, of course, because there's nothing to be done about those big boulders. It's backbreaking work when we have to clear the ground of the smaller stones.

Beyond that, over that brown furrow, are my olive orchards, and that yellow patch beneath is some barley I planted in the spring – it's come up well.

Over there on the right is the grain land and up there on that small hillock is our threshing ground. Those fields over there belong to my brothers. I've got two sons myself and how they are going to manage with only half between them I don't know . . . but that's the law of inheritance for you. Luckily the gods spared us when the Spartans invaded. The village over the hill was devastated and it takes a good 30 years to

BEASTS OF BURDEN An affluent farmer, modelled in terracotta, has two oxen to draw his plough.

grow a really fruitful olive tree. I can't imagine what it must feel like to have to leave your family graves and break up the household like some of the farmers there have had to do.

I've got my own worries. The farm looks good now, but last year was terrible for us. The crops all failed and my well dried up so there wasn't a vegetable in the garden – I thought we were going to starve. As it was, I had to get a loan of grain from a big farmer nearby and now I'm not certain I can repay him on time. And what then? He'll take my land and then I'll be like those others I was telling you about – deprived of my ancestors and maybe forced to work for another man like labourers out for hire – no better than a slave. Maybe we can sell the ox? The mule can draw the cart . . . What will I do? This is my home, my city, my kingdom.

The plough drawn by oxen or mules with a separate share (cutting blade) was capable only of furrowing the top soil. The work had to be finished off with a spade or hoe. Hesiod had detailed advice on all such matters including the best animals to draw a plough: 'Get two nine-year-old bull oxen. In their prime, they have full strength, and work the best, nor will they quarrel in the furrows, break the plough, and leave the work unfinished.'

He was equally precise in his advice about farm hands: 'After [the oxen] should go a vigorous 40-year-old hand, who'll dine upon a quartered, eight-slice loaf.' A mature worker like this would 'do his job and drive the furrows straight'. He would 'keep his mind on work, not look around for friends, the way a young man would. He'll sow with care, not wasting seed; less stable men get flustered, dreaming of their social life.'

Sowing was done by hand and reaping with a one-handled sickle. The farmer had to have his back to the wind when reaping to stop the grain being blown into his face. The cut sheaves were then

GATHERING IN THE HARVEST Olive pickers use poles – and one even clambers up into a tree – to shake the fruit to the ground. Olives were gathered in November and the oil was extracted in presses (right).

laid out on a stone or packed-earth threshing floor and trampled by a team of mules rotating around a central post on a long rope – the wind blew the chaff away. From the 4th century BC onwards, agricultural experts began to study crop rotation but little was achieved in practice beyond the recognition that land must be left fallow from time to time.

The main crop in most of Greece was the olive which, with its long roots and narrow leaves, was well adapted to the arid conditions – the long roots allow the olive tree to tap whatever water is available; the narrow leaves prevent undue evaporation of moisture. Olives were either harvested by hand or else beaten down with rods. They were then pulverised in a kind of mortar with a hole at the bottom through which the oil trickled, leaving the debris for use as fertiliser or to work into wood or leather.

Appropriately, the grape harvest was performed to the sound of the flute and involved much ribaldry and drunkenness. It came in September when, according to Hesiod (monitoring the seasons, as was customary, by the passage of the constellations across the heavens), 'Orion and the Dog Star move into the mid-sky, and Arcturus sees the rosy-fingered Dawn. . . .'

PRINCELY LANDOWNERS
In most city-states wealth and social standing were based on land, with a number of big country estates surviving well into the 5th century BC and after. Among the very largest were those belonging

107

PAINTING HERACLES Originally Greek sculpture was painted. Here an artist applies layers of wax paint to a statue of Heracles.

for them by slaves. Surplus income was never channelled back into the land to make it more productive. The prestige which large landholding implied, even in democratic states, was what mattered most.

CRAFTSMEN AS ARTISTS

There was no word for artist in the language of the ancient Greeks. From sculptor to potter, such people were all known as craftsmen. That did not stop them from taking pride in their work and inscribing their names on statues or painted vases for future generations to see. But they were never likely to experiment with individual artistic self-expression. The success of a piece of work depended on how lifelike the audience judged it to be. Pheidias, the Athenian sculptor, hid himself within earshot of spectators who came to see his statue of Zeus and altered it according to their comments.

Manufacture amounted to myriad cottage industries manned by individual specialists and their small groups of assistant slaves, all using the minimum of technological expertise. Throughout the 5th century when Athens, along with Corinth, dominated the trade in high-quality pottery in Greece, only 500 potters were working in the city.

On the other hand, Athens needed hundreds, if not thousands, of different artisans to meet its other various needs – whether it was sculpting pediments for the Parthenon or building triremes. The state provided the raw materials for public works and then divided up the tasks among the craftsmen and their assistants, along with sundry unskilled labourers and slaves – all working alongside each other. Pericles calculated that the large-scale construction projects he planned for the Parthenon would need men from 22 different trades, and thus guaranteed steady work for large numbers of people.

to the nobles of Thessaly in the north of Greece who maintained households and retinues of princely munificence. They included figures such as Meno of Pharsalus, able to raise 300 cavalrymen from among his serfs to fight alongside the Athenians in 476 BC.

On a more modest scale, Xenophon, a substantial Athenian landowner, described his own fertile acres 'watered by the Selinous river . . . which abounds both in fish and shellfish'. He had well-stocked hunting grounds together with fruit orchards, 'meadowland, and low tree-clad hills suitable for the raising of pigs, goats, cattle, and indeed horses'. The statesman Pericles was a typical absentee landlord who delegated the supervision of work on his lands to a slave-bailiff and used the income to defray the costs of life in the city.

Although 45 to 70 acre (18 to 28 ha) holdings – fairly large by Attic standards – were not unusual, the Athenian rich tended to have numerous smaller farms scattered around the countryside which they might rent out lucratively to tenants or have worked

MAKING MUSIC An apprentice lyre-maker fixes strings to a tortoiseshell base. The lyre was the most important instrument in Greek music.

used a coarse brush to paint the background black (or white if it was a funeral urn) so that the figures stood out in the natural reddish colour of the clay. The black glaze had a fine metallic sheen and was very long lasting.

Sometimes, the potters also made terracotta statuettes needed in large quantities for dedication to the gods and the dead. The larger terracotta statues which stood on the tops and outside corners of the pediments of temples and tombs were made by sculptors who otherwise worked in stone or bronze.

For metalworkers, temperatures in their smithies could reach intolerable levels, with the men stripped to work. The 6 ft (1.8 m) brick furnaces were lined with clay and banded round for extra strength. Layers of charcoal and ore were lit with kindling, the door closed and a blast sent up the tower with goatskin bellows. The heat was maintained by closing the top of the furnace. The melted ore trickled down in a lump to the bottom of the furnace where it was retrieved, reheated and hammered into shape.

IN TRADE

In Athens, the metics (resident aliens) monopolised most of the retail trade, thanks to the stigma that Athenians attached to being middlemen.

The bulk of the city's export and import trade, too, was

Work began early in the morning and continued until sunset. As Aristophanes put it: 'When the cock sings his dawn song, up they all spring and hurry off to work – coppersmiths, potters, shoemakers, tanners, bathmen, millers, lyre-makers-cum-shield-turners; why, some of them are shod and abroad when it's still quite dark.' The men often sang as they worked or performed their tasks to the rhythm set by a flute player.

Potters turned out a huge variety of different artefacts – both practical and decorative – on a crude flat wheel rotated by hand on an upright spindle. The pot was hardened in the sun, polished, decorated and finally baked in a clay oven. Vase painters sketched their drawings on the pot and then

THE WOODWORKER'S ART A carpenter holds a piece of wood between his knees as he gets to work with a long-handled hammer.

STRIPPED FOR ACTION   **A bronzesmith stokes the furnace while a colleague (on the right) assembles a statue.**

in the hands of foreign merchants, usually non-residents. They bought cargoes of Athenian-made goods with small sums of money loaned to them by Athenian citizens or metics at exorbitant rates (up to 120 per cent). The lenders were not necessarily rich and the sums of money involved were often comparatively small. Those who loaned the largest sums were usually metics who were not allowed to buy land with any surplus money as most Athenian citizens preferred to do. The merchants shipped the goods to other city-states, sold them and then repaid their loans when they were next in Athens.

It was a high-risk venture given the vagaries of currents and piracy, but it could also be extremely profitable. This made it attractive to those who, as Hesiod had put it in the 8th century BC, were 'longing to flee from debts and painful want. . .'. But as Hesiod also pointed out to his brother Perses, speculators should take certain basic precautions: '. . . Perses, keep in mind that all works have their proper seasons: sailing, most of all. Admire small ships, but put your cargo in a big one, for a larger cargo brings a larger profit, if the storms hold off.' The same principle held true in the 5th century.

The slow, wide trading boats were sail-powered and could achieve a maximum speed of 5 knots (6 mph – 10 km/h). Equipped with food and water to last them for several days, the small crews had no need to put into shore. The traders were often paid in kind at their port of destination. Alternatively, the Athenian silver coinage, which was famous for its purity, could be weighed and exchanged as bullion.

During the 5th century, Piraeus became the commercial centre of the eastern Mediterranean because the Athenians had the boats to transport goods and Athens itself provided a large market. The various Greek colonies scattering the shores of the Mediterranean and Black Sea provided a natural market for export. At the same time, a huge variety of different goods from abroad passed through Athens. They ranged from luxury items such as frankincense from Syria to wood from Thrace, used in Athenian warships. Customs duties were levied by the Athenians at 1, then 2, per cent of the value of merchandise passing through the port.

Above all, Athens relied on imported grain to supplement its own crops. It produced enough grain to feed only a quarter of its population in the

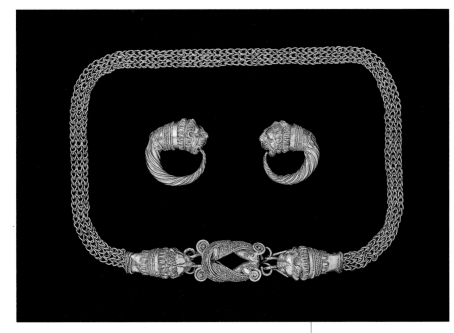

FEMININE ADORNMENTS
The fine craftsmanship of
Greek goldsmiths is seen
in a necklace and earrings
of the 3rd century BC.

over the next 150 years. Some were established as trading posts but in most cases the needs of land-hungry, expanding populations helped to drive settlers from rocky homelands to seek more fertile territories abroad. In the process, they founded many cities that exist to this day.

The fruitful plains of Sicily and southern Italy, ideal for growing grain, had an obvious appeal, and numerous Greek communities sprouted along their coasts. The Corinthians founded Syracuse in Sicily. In southern Italy, the Achaeans from the northern Peloponnese founded Sybaris and Croton (modern Crotone), while the Spartans established Taras (Taranto). Traders from the Ionian city of Phocaea ventured farther afield when they established colonies in southern Gaul at Massilia (Marseilles), Nicaea (Nice) and Antipolis (Antibes). Settlers from the volcanic crag of Thera (Santorini) founded Cyrene on the North African coast, while Megara (in central Greece) and Miletus (on the Turkish coast) led the way through the Bosporus and along the Black Sea coasts as far as Trapezus (Trabzon) and Phasis in the east and the Crimea in the north.

The original colonising group was usually quite small, perhaps 200 or 300 men – they would probably have married among the women of the region's native population. The leader came from the city sponsoring the expedition, but many of his followers might come from other cities.

Inevitably patterns of settlement varied from colony to colony, but in many cases land was

5th century and the population doubled in the 4th. The need to control the grain supply was vital and Athens was able to do so because of its supremacy at sea. The extent of its control is shown by a decree of 426 BC allowing Methone on the Thermaic Gulf in the northern Aegean to import a fixed amount of grain annually from Byzantium upon registering with the Athenian officials there. These officials, with the backing of the navy if necessary, could deny any Greek city access to the Black Sea and thus to the main sea route not only for grain but for slaves, hides and other crucial products.

LIFE IN THE COLONIES

The Greek colonies had greatly increased the scope for trade. The first had been Naxos on the Strait of Messina between Sicily and the toe of Italy – founded in 734 BC by settlers from Chalcis on the island of Euboea north of Attica. Many others followed

PRECIOUS URNS   Silver mined by slaves in Attica's Laurium mines could be moulded into luxury pots like these.

allotted in more or less equal portions before the colonising expedition set out. In many of the Sicilian and Italian colonies, each settler was given a rectangular plot large enough for a house and a substantial garden around it – making the new cities much more open and spacious than their crowded counterparts in the Greek homelands. These plots were neatly laid out within the city walls, while the farming land outside the walls was shared out in an equally orderly fashion. In most cases the first settlers and their descendants became the colony's aristocracy.

Once founded, the colony was independent of its mother city, though it usually maintained close cultural ties. Any attempt at a permanent return to the mother city was strongly discouraged. Stories of the founding of Cyrene around 630 BC tell how the Theran colonisers at first lost their nerve when confronted with the place they were destined to settle, and so turned back for home.

But their kinsmen had no intention of letting them get away with such spineless conduct. They 'stoned them as they were putting in', according to the historian Herodotus, 'and would not allow them to land, telling them to sail back again' – which the colonisers duly did. Like many such expeditions, the Cyrenean one had received the official blessing of the Delphic oracle, and this would have made settlers' commitment to the enterprise all the more sacrosanct.

THE LIFE OF A SLAVE

It was slave labour that freed the Greek citizen to pursue his civic and military duties, with the slaves coming from a variety of sources. Greek men and women risked slavery through being captured in time of war. Babies left to die of exposure were occasionally picked up to be reared as slaves. But the main supply of human livestock was in the hand of professional dealers trading in slaves from non-Greek peoples to the north and east; the slaves obtained in this way included Phrygians, Thracians and Syrians. Supply was plentiful and cheap and all but the poorest Greeks owned a slave. A cripple who argued in an Athenian court that he was eligible for state relief remarked that he was too poor even to buy a slave.

Athenian slaves were bought at monthly auctions held in the market place. Prices depended on skills. The master gave his slave a name (often a derivative

MONEY AND USURY

NO ONE knows for sure how to calculate the modern equivalents of ancient Greek currency.

The island of Aegina was the first of the Greek states to coin currency some time around 600 BC. Then Athens followed suit in about 570.

The high-denomination coins were made of silver. They included the silver drachma which was used for the kind of business for which we would use a cheque. One drachma was equivalent to 6 silver obols. Small brass currency or barter was used as the means of exchange in everyday transactions.

People buried their hoards of money at home. Even Athenian state treasurers kept their cash in coffers which they dipped into whenever an official needed to be paid. Bankers were rare, usually slaves or metics, and no more than currency exchangers or pawnbrokers who lent out money for a pledge. Land-secured debts were the most common kind of loan. If the debtor defaulted on the deal he forfeited his property.

MAKING A MINT Emblems on coins included the king's head in Greek-ruled Bactria in central Asia (top left), a shield in Thebes, the ruler's wife in Syracuse and a bee (associated with the goddess Artemis) in Ephesus.

LOADING CARGO Trade thrived among the Greek cities and colonies of the Mediterranean and the Black Sea.

of the slave's place of origin, such as Thratta for a Thracian) and could beat or maim him or her at will. Slaves were chattels (objects) which could be sold, hired out or given as a pledge on a debt, and had no rights whatsoever. They were not educated, although they did worship together with their masters and could be buried in their plots.

Kindly masters allowed slaves to breed together as a means of securing their loyalty. They would not otherwise have gone to the expense of rearing them, when to buy an adult slave cost the equivalent of one year's keep. Others might brand a runaway slave with a red-hot iron. Flogging was allowed by law as a means of goading a slave into action, as it was with a recalcitrant mule. But in practice, many slave-owners seem to have been fairly humane. As the Athenian Xenophon put it: 'Slaves need the stimulus of good hopes even more than free men to make them steadfast.'

Slaves worked in the house or on the land alongside their master or mistress; the vital distinction between them was in the slaves' lack of freedom. In most households, the relationship was a familiar one, given the cramped nature of Greek houses and the garrulous character of the Greeks themselves.

City-dwellers sometimes delegated an entire business to a slave, allowing him to set up home where he wished so long as he paid his master a proportion of what he earned. Some slaves earned enough to buy back their freedom. A diligent bank clerk called Pasion was not only freed but went on to make an enormous fortune. Even more remarkably, he eventually acquired Athenian citizenship. Very occasionally, in a military crisis, slaves were freed to fight in the army or

FACE VASE This finely crafted Athenian vase is evidence of the cosmopolitan mix in Athens.

113

SMALL WORLD **This Ethiopian warrior is depicted on a 6th-century BC Greek amphora. Trade and war alike encouraged contact with other peoples.**

navy. Large slave owners like the Athenian Nicias who owned 1000 might hire them out to others. Many ended up working in the mines at Laurium.

The only Greek enterprise that could be called an industry in anything like the modern sense was the silver mines at Laurium. These were worked by 10 000 (at fullest capacity perhaps 30 000) slaves. The slaves worked in appalling conditions, using rudimentary tools in narrow galleries dimly illuminated by smoky oil lamps. Above ground, the silver ore was smelted, giving off poisonous fumes which killed off all the surrounding vegetation. It was by the smelting plant that the slaves camped at night.

Finally, in Athens, there were state-owned slaves who were paid a salary and lived where they chose. They performed jobs as clerks for the Council and Assembly, in the law courts and in the police force of 1000 Scythian archers. The state-executioner, too, was a slave, as were the street sweepers and skilled workers in the Mint.

HELOTS AND MANHUNTS

According to the Athenian Critias, Spartan slaves were more fully slaves than their counterparts anywhere else. Spartan helots, descended from the region's original inhabitants, lived on the land and had to render half of their produce to their masters. Although they were state-owned rather than the property of individual masters and could live family lives on their ancestral lands, they were subject to regular cullings and savage manhunts perpetrated by Spartan youth groups.

Little is known about what the slaves thought of their status, but in 413 when the Spartans were camped outside the Athenian walls, 20 000 slaves deserted to the enemy despite what must have seemed an extremely uncertain future. Indeed, at all times, runaway slaves were a common domestic problem for the Greeks. Equally, however, some household slaves – in particular, nurses and the pedagogues who looked after Athenian schoolboys – grew strongly attached to their masters. Certainly, slaves would not have criticised the institution of slavery itself. When they revolted their aim was to return to their native countries or to enslave their masters in their turn.

OUTNUMBERED BY SLAVES

There were about 80 000-100 000 slaves in Athens at the time of its greatest prosperity, which was also when its population was largest. This means that there was an average of one and a half slaves per citizen.

SLAVE FOR LIFE **A slave boy follows behind his Athenian owner. In Athens, unlike Sparta with its slave race of helots, most slaves came from abroad.**

THE GREEKS AT PLAY

The Greeks played as hard as they worked – and with the same competitive spirit.

Runners (like those above) were among the sportsmen who competed at

the Olympic Games and other, more local events. Similarly, dramatists

wrote and produced plays in competition, openly taunting each other

in their zeal to come first. The big festivals, such as Athens' Panathenaea,

were magnificent occasions, drawing people from all over Greece.

DRAMA AND ATHLETICS

Greek festivals were bustling, extravagant affairs, with music, processions, races,

religious rituals, feasting and drinking. Out of this ferment arose the great Athenian tragedies

and comedies and the achievements of Olympic athletes from all over the Greek lands.

THE ANCIENT Greeks were good at entertaining themselves while at the same time worshipping their gods. Their great public festivals, which were always religious occasions, were glorious events that combined dramatic and athletic contests with ribaldry, carousing and highly serious ritual. In Athens magnificent processions wound their way up to the Acropolis involving everyone from the people designated to carry sacred objects to the ordinary citizen bearing an olive branch. Such celebrations, including the competitive events, were believed to delight the gods every bit as much as their mortal servants.

One of the greatest of them was Athens' Panathenaea, which was held annually but celebrated with particular magnificence every four years when it drew citizens from throughout Attica and beyond. It included a torch race in which brands were lit at Eros's altar in the Academy (an olive grove outside the city walls). The torches were then raced in relay teams to the goddess Athena's altar on the Acropolis, where the winner kindled a sacred fire.

The next day a procession of priests, officials and soldiers on horseback wearing purple cloaks headed a large crowd as they made their way through the city to the Acropolis. They dragged with them a ship's mast on wheels with a new gown for the statue of Athena draped over it. After the procession, the entire city feasted on the meat of sacrificial cows while potters moved among crowds selling souvenir wine jars. The noise was terrific as the people ate, drank and applauded the

MUSIC MAKER A lyre's sound box consisted of a tortoise shell with leather stretched over it.

winners of the musical and athletic contests who were now awarded their prizes – jars of olive oil made from trees sacred to Athena. Others crowded around solo singers accompanied by the flute or lyre and orators competing against each other with renditions from the *Iliad* and the *Odyssey*.

In some festivals the participants were exclusively female. At the Athenian feast of Demeter Thesmophoria, held in honour of the goddess of fertility, Demeter, the fruitfulness of both crops and women was encouraged by a ceremony performed by married women only. This included the use of phallic symbols made of pastry. Phallic displays were, in fact, part of all Greek fertility festivals – whether they were lined up to look like corn stalks and sprinkled with seed by courtesans or paraded through the fields at a country Dionysia festival behind a girl basket-bearer.

A country Dionysia was an uproarious occasion in honour of Dionysus, the god of wine, during which peasants tried

PLAY ON This terracotta maiden from the 3rd century BC plays a lute-like instrument.

RIBALD FUN An actor playing Hermes leads the chorus in a satyr play, providing lighter relief after three tragedies.

to balance on inflated wineskins and drunkards roamed the town or village streets dancing, singing and aiming obscene jokes at anyone who crossed their paths. Athens itself had such festivals including the Anthesteria in early spring. Jars of wine, stored since the autumn, were cracked open and gulped down in drinking competitions. When a trumpet sounded, each reveller had to swallow a potful of wine as quickly as possible. The city's chief magistrate was dressed as Dionysus and paraded through the streets on a boat-shaped float.

DRAMAS FOR DIONYSUS

Athens had two other festivals in honour of Dionysus – the Great (or City) Dionysia in March and the Lenaea in January. Both included competitively performed plays. A set number of playwrights was chosen by a board of officials who had themselves been selected randomly by lot. Lacking expertise, the selectors tended to favour the big names among the playwrights. The dramas were performed in an atmosphere of intense rivalry for the coveted prize of a myrtle wreath awarded by a jury of ten men – one from each of the tribes into which the Athenian population was divided – again chosen by lot.

The plays were extremely popular, attended by huge numbers of ordinary Athenian citizens, who were probably ignorant of the other intellectual achievements of their time, as well as by visiting foreigners and metics. Each set of plays had a one-day showing after which they might be performed again in rural areas.

The actors were professionals, and all male – women's parts were played by men. Particularly good actors were eagerly sought out by playwrights who usually produced their plays themselves. They had to be extremely versatile – with as many as 18 parts shared out among three or four actors – and were paid by the state.

Rich citizens financed dramatic productions, undertaking to pay for the costumes and training of the chorus. This was, in fact, a kind of taxation, a civic obligation imposed on the rich.

At dawn on the first day of the festival, people made their way to the theatre. They were ready for four days of acting, in which they would see as many as 17 different productions. All citizens received a grant so that they could attend free. They scrabbled for a good place on the semi-circular rocky slopes, covered with wooden seats, which rose up from the 66 ft (20 m) circular 'dancing area' (*orchestra*) – the stone-seated amphitheatres surviving today were not built until the 4th century BC. Officials and honoured guests took the front places. Boys, slaves and foreigners found standing room wherever they could.

The ceremony began with a ritual purification, after which an official drew lots to decide the order in which the plays would be performed. People whistled and heckled as each playwright's name was announced. Then the plays began.

The acoustics were usually very good, so that even the people in the back rows could hear well-trained actors. At the same

SERIOUS RECREATION This girl plays the *kithara*, a version of the lyre with a wooden sound box.

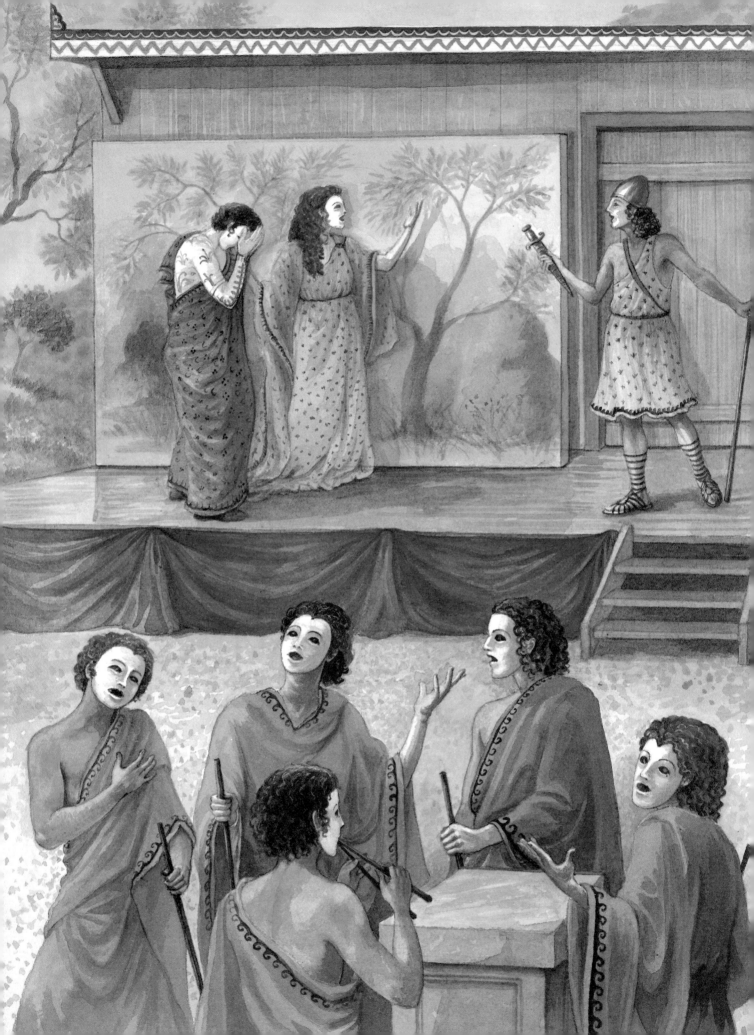

DRAMATIC LOCATION The theatre at Dodona in north-western Greece (right) was dedicated to Zeus. These ruins date mostly from the 3rd century BC. Opposite: all-male actors enact a tragedy on a small stage backed by simple scenery. The figures in the foreground are the chorus who comment on the action.

time, the actors used extravagant gestures and wore brightly coloured clothes that helped to make their movements visible to the more distant parts of the audience. They had shoes with specially thick soles and huge masks to magnify the features of the characters they portrayed. They wore wigs to add to their height and padded their bodies to increase their girth. They told the audience of the emotions they were experiencing – anything more subtle than the declaration 'I weep' or 'I laugh' would have passed the spectators by.

They performed on a low stage at the back of the dancing floor behind which stood a flat-topped building. This had a central door through which they entered and exited as well as at the sides of the stage.

Scenery was rudimentary. Generally the Greeks were content to listen to the speeches of the actors with few props. Among those that did exist was a crane fixed on the flat roof which swung heroes and deities into action from a rope. In one of Aristophanes' comic plays a character proceeds to heaven on the back of a giant dung beetle: 'Oh dear, I'm scared – I'm not joking now! Crane-man, do pay attention to what you're doing with me! I'm beginning to get collywobbles, and if you're not careful I'll be giving the beetle a meal!'

A chorus, which for a tragedy comprised 15 men, sang, danced and soliloquised from the dancing floor in front of the actor's stage. They were the stage audience who commented upon the unfolding events for the clarification of the real audience.

Although other civilisations had staged dramatic productions in one form or another, the Greeks were the first to write serious, powerful plays about people and their emotions. Unfolding slowly and formally, and expressed in lyrical language, the Greek tragedies, like Homer's epics, took their themes from myths – the destruction of a hero or superman – with which the whole audience was familiar. At Athens' Great Dionysia festival, each tragic playwright competed with a quartet of plays performed in sequence. The first three plays were tragedies with a common plot running through them; the last was a satyr play to bring light relief.

THE FATHER OF TRAGEDY

Aeschylus, the first of the great tragedians whose plays have survived, penned, among many other works, a trilogy of plays known as the *Oresteia*, based on the mythical story of Orestes, son of Agamemnon, the Greek leader during the Trojan wars.

Everyone in the audience knew what was going to happen. In the first play, Agamemnon, who before setting out for Troy had slaughtered his own child in order to procure a favourable wind for his journey, would be murdered by Clytemnestra, his adulterous wife, to avenge her daughter's death. Then, in the second play, Agamemnon's son Orestes would retaliate by killing his mother; in the third, Orestes

LEADER OF THE PACK A vase painting shows the leader of the chorus displaying his mask during a satyr play.

119

AXE PLAY Agamemnon's wife Clytemnestra hacks to death his concubine Cassandra. The story of Agamemnon inspired several Greek tragedies.

The great names of Greek tragedy were Aeschylus, Sophocles and Euripides. Aeschylus (*c.*525-456 BC) fought the Persians at Marathon (490) and Salamis (480). During his lifetime he saw his native Athens transformed from a tyranny into a democracy. He also had contacts with the Greek communities of Sicily, notably the court of the tyrant Hieron of Syracuse. They were eventful years and Aeschylus was evidently a close observer of all that was happening around him, especially the dilemmas facing political leaders. The conflicting calls of public duty and personal affections in figures such as Agamemnon are a common theme in his plays.

As a youth Sophocles (*c.*495-406 BC) was a skilled athlete and musician; he was also regarded as one of the most beautiful young men of his generation. As a result he was chosen, aged 16, to play a leading part in the celebrations following the Athenian victory at Salamis. When he was 28 years old he beat Aeschylus at Athens' Great Dionysia. He was still writing in his eighties in 406 when he composed a chorus in mourning for Euripides, who was ten years his junior. Only seven of his 100 or more plays

INEBRIATED WIT Drunkenness and physical ugliness were the themes for much knock-about fun in Greek comedy.

would be acquitted by the goddess Athena and in this way he would bring the long cycle of curses on the royal house to an end.

The Greeks were happy to watch different interpretations of the same myths again and again – frequently hissing their disapproval at newfangled music or barracking a bad actor. It was from these myths, after all, that they derived their precepts for living. The myths formed their literary heritage and were what made them Greek.

At the same time, the great playwrights depicted their heroes and gods as figures with whom the audience could identify, troubling them with emotions which we can still share today. All the issues that were important to the Greeks – the relationships between gods and men, the sanctity of the household, the mistreatment of parents, murder and revenge – were dramatised, employing the new techniques people of the 5th century BC were acquiring. These included the honed rhetorical skills of the Athenian courtroom or Assembly, the use of energetic debate to discuss abstract qualities such as virtue and evil and the analysis of what makes people behave as they do.

survive, including *Oedipus Rex*, *Oedipus at Colonus* and *Antigone*.

Euripides (*c*.480-406) was first selected to take part in a dramatic festival in 455 and brought off his first victory 14 years later in 441 – the play has not survived. He spent the last two years of his life at the court of the Macedonian king. Tradition has it that his marriage to a women named Melito was unhappy, but there is no positive proof of this. He did, however, make something of a speciality of portraying women driven by destructive, often

SUBLIME TO RIDICULOUS
The terracotta masks worn by tragic and comic actors denoted mood as well as character.

treacherous, impulses. Among the most famous of his surviving works are *The Trojan Women*, *Medea* and *Iphigenia in Tauris*.

During the comparatively short period of 70 years between the performance of Aeschylus' first surviving play in 472 BC and the posthumous

THE CUTTHROAT WORLD OF PLAYWRITING

HORSE PLAY The antics of the chorus – sometimes involving animals, from horses to wasps – were a high point for the audiences of Greek comedy.

THE PLAYWRIGHT Aristophanes first broke into the dramatic limelight in 427 BC. That year he came second in Athens' Great Dionysia festival with his first play *The Banqueters*. He followed this up the next year with *The Babylonians* which came first and won him the coveted ivy wreath. It also incited the wrath of the demagogue Cleon who took him to court on the grounds that he had discredited Athens. Aristophanes never forgot Cleon's attack and the next four plays were remarkable for the vitriolic criticism he levelled at the politician – the most vicious play of all being *The Knights*, in which Cleon was the chief protagonist.

Aristophanes liked to win at the Great Dionysia and frequently used his plays as weapons against rivals. In *The Clouds* he claimed that another playwright, Eupolis, had plagiarised *The Knights*. Eupolis responded with the claim that he had helped Aristophanes to write the play without demanding any kind of fee. Another victim was the playwright Cratinus, who had actually produced three of Aristophanes' own works. This did not prevent Aristophanes from vilifying him as a washed-up alcoholic. Cratinus neatly responded at the next festival by portraying himself as, indeed, a washed-up alcoholic but one who argued that only such a figure could produce anything that was worthwhile. The audience agreed with him and he came first while Aristophanes came third.

Beyond the jokes and linguistic gymnastics, Aristophanes had important issues to communicate to his audience. He was an Athenian patriot who, though he had no time for pacifism, was intolerant of politicians who continued wars over trifles when peace was easily attainable. He was also a democrat, but one who despised the people when they gave power to demagogues like Cleon.

showing of Sophocles' *Oedipus at Colonus* in 401 BC, actors and characterisation in Athenian tragedies became more human and realistic, but even so the audience remained at a remove. After the aloof dignity of the tragedies the involvement of the audience in Attic comedy must have seemed like pantomime after the opera.

COMIC RELIEF

Officially comedies began in 486 – when for the first time a comic playwright had his name carved on the stone recording victors at the Great Dionysia, previously monopolised by the writers of tragedy. But comedies had been performed in some form or another ever since their origin in ancient fertility processions.

Of the 700 titles we know about, only the plays of Aristophanes have survived. Taking the point of view of the middle-class farmer, Aristophanes mocked and chastised all strata of society. Nobody and nothing was sacrosanct. All the political figures of the day, major and minor, were depicted as vain, greedy and corrupt and wherever possible represented as ugly, vulgar, perverted and of dubious citizen status. The suspicious Attic farmer had all his fears confirmed when ostentatiously dressed generals were shown fleeing from the battlefield or intellectual figures like Socrates tied themselves into knots with futile or downright immoral arguments, while the 'real' men were out exercising in the gym. Not even the gods were immune from ridicule. In one play Dionysus faints from terror and soils himself; in the same play his intellect and virile qualities are so inferior to those

GREEK GLOVES Boxers wear the bandage-like strips of cloth known as *himantes*.

STRIPPED FOR ACTION In Sparta, unlike other states, girls took a full part in athletics. Their short tunics provoked ribald comments from other Greeks.

of his slave that master and dependant exchange status. For once, the tables could be turned on the gods who played skittles with mortal lives.

There was something in the comedies for everybody. Mockery of the 'stupid' way foreigners talked and gross sexual jokes appealed as much to children and peasants as to the more educated members of the audience. All but the illiterate recognised that it was Aeschylus who was being sent up when passages of highfalutin obscurity occurred. But only the most highly educated would have caught the full range of literary references Aristophanes played with. Aristophanes was also concerned with serious issues – such as peace or the democracy of Athens – which he dealt with using a solemn lyricism that went straight to the heart of the patriotic citizen. Such a citizen would also have recognised the myriad references to topical affairs – often requiring last-minute rewrites.

Typically, comic playwrights began with a prologue in which the actors clowned around before introducing the plot. The arrival of the chorus might be spectacular – bursting in as birds or clouds in two of Aristophanes' plays. Then came the main action in which the chorus often began by opposing the actors in argument and song. The audience accepted the non sequiturs, sudden flights into the supernatural or appearances of personified

THE DIVER A wall painting from the Greek city of Paestum in Italy shows a man diving from a special platform.

abstracts like Poverty without demur, as they did the fantastical ideas around which the narrative revolved. In Aristophanes' *Lysistra*, for instance, the women go on sexual strike against their husbands to force them to make peace – even though all the men are beyond temptation on the battlefield.

THE COMPETITIVE SPIRIT

In ancient times, it would have been the duels of warlike heroes that provided the outlet for the Greeks' intensely competitive spirit and their need for public glory. After hoplite fighting transformed warfare, leaving a lesser role for the individual hero, sport fulfilled much the same function. The various Panhellenic festivals, common to all Greeks, allowed athletes to excel and rich men to spend fortunes marketing themselves while also honouring their gods.

Every four years, thousands of people from all over the Greek-speaking world gathered in a temporary camp at Olympia sheltering under Mount Cronus in the western Peloponnese. They had come to see the greatest of their athletes perform in honour of Zeus. This was always first and foremost a religious festival, and even when states were engaged in one of their interminable wars people travelling to or from the games were left unharmed in otherwise hostile territory – this safeguard lasted

LONG JUMP Naked athletes use stone or metal weights, known as *halters* (left), to help to propel them through the air. Their landing points were marked with pegs. The long jump was the only jumping event in Greek games.

a month. The people who came farthest were aristocrats who enjoyed fraternising between events with their counterparts from elsewhere.

The first day was dedicated to religious ritual and a few boys' events. All the competitors sacrificed to the gods and swore that they had been properly trained and would not cheat. These rites were focused on the Altis or 'sacred grove of Zeus', dominated after about 460 BC by a huge Temple of Zeus. It housed a superb gold and ivory statue of the god created by the Athenian sculptor Phidias and reckoned to be one of the 'seven wonders of the world'.

Then the four main days of sporting competition began. The athletes performed naked, limbering up beforehand in the gymnasium or wrestling school and making full use of the plunge baths, basins, saunas and anointing rooms which constituted the equivalent of modern leisure centres. The main programme opened with chariot and horse races. They were the most glorious events of all, dominated by the aristocracy who were the only people rich enough to run horses, though they usually had slaves to drive the chariots or ride the horses for them – rather like modern race-horse

EQUESTRIAN SPORT An Attic vase of the 6th century BC shows a charioteer urging on his four-horse team.

A DAY IN THE LIFE OF

A VICTOR AT THE CORINTHIAN GAMES

I COULD SCARCELY believe it when my trainer came to me and said that I had been chosen to compete for our city Thebes in the running. I was to be let off military service to practise for the games and would only return to barracks after it was all over. I ran every morning after that, pushing myself to exceed the previous day's speed, and exercising in the afternoon to hone my muscles further. On the day of our departure I looked over at my father as I stood with the priests, officials and athletes – both men and boys – and understood the expression of anxious pride upon his face.

My first sight of marble-clad Corinth was unforgettable. Even the baths and dressing rooms allotted to us were sculpted from the finest marble. The Council of the Games read us the rules and showed everyone to his lodgings as well as the room where we would all eat. The stadium was filled with my competitors – all running, running, running – completely oblivious to the crowds of peddlers touting good-luck charms and pimps whispering the delights of the city's brothels.

WINNER TAKES ALL An athlete is bedecked with a wreath and ribbons – all tokens of victory.

When I had finished my day's practice, I wandered along streets which were packed with stalls selling everything from oil to costly silver jewels – things I could never afford. There were men swallowing swords, others juggling lighted torches and singers quarrelling over prime sites for their performances. At every step there was something new to be seen if you could make your way through the crowds. It was here, while I was watching all the bustle that a man approached me with a bribe not to win. Although I had heard of such

deals being struck on behalf of big gamblers I found myself shaking from the shock. How could anyone accept money in preference to glory?

After three days of hard training the day arrived. Even before dawn I could hear the rumble of the early-comers arriving to get the best seats and this had risen to a roar by the time I made my way to the dressing room. Touts, water-sellers and men trading in cakes or ribbons shouted their wares above the throng. I watched the boys' races in a stupor and then the tumblers and flute players came out and I knew it was my time. I can remember nothing about that run except the dust in my eyes, the sharp pain in my side and the final god-given spurt which launched me ahead of the last man in front of me. As I hit the finishing post I thought I was being lynched but it was myrtle wreaths being flung at my face and body. Only when I fixed the winning ribbons around my head did I fully realise that I had won. The next day I processed to the temple with the others and was crowned before Poseidon. Two days later I was back in Thebes.

owners. The young Athenian aristocrat Alcibiades entered nine chariots for the chariot race in the games of 416, coming first, second and fourth.

The pentathlon consisted of running, jumping, discus-throwing, javelin-throwing and wrestling, watched by the vast audience sitting on the earth banks of the stadium. There were four running races: the 200 yd (180 m) sprint, the quarter-mile

(400 m), the 'long haul' of approximately 2 miles (3 km) and the race in armour. The competitors raced up and down, not round as we do, a white-sand track. Starting and finishing posts were marked by stones 18 in (46 cm) wide, with grooves cut into the starting point to give the runner a launching foothold – those who started too soon risked a beating from the umpire's rod.

The long jump was performed with the help of two weights which the athlete used to propel himself over the ploughed-up ground; his landing was marked by a little peg. The discus thrower held a metal plate above his head before swinging it backwards and launching it as far as he could with all his body weight behind him. The javelin thrower gripped the leather thong in the middle of a spear that was longer than he was tall. Finally, there was the *pankration*, a peculiarly brutal competition, in which two men fought in any way they knew – strangling, arm-twisting or jumping up and down on each other. They were only debarred from gouging out one another's eyes and biting.

A herald announced the names of the winners of all the events – glorious beings who were rewarded by a simple olive crown. One town, determined to honour its returning hero properly, tore down a section of the fortified walls so that he might enter without treading where lesser men had walked. An Olympic victory was the highest prize to which a man could aspire.

HEAVY ASSETS
Metal tripods were among the prizes at contests – like cups at modern championships.

By the 4th century BC, however, things had started to change. The specialist athlete had taken over, training elaborately and eating large quantities of meat to produce the top-heavy body that was deemed unsuitable for warfare but particularly good for sport. The Spartans forbade this sort of training and their citizens, once predominant among the Olympic victors, no longer competed.

GLORIOUS CROWN   Records of an athlete's triumphs went with him to his grave. This commemorative wreath made from beaten gold would never have been worn. Instead it was buried with the former athlete when he died.

MIND, BODY AND SPIRIT

For most people in ancient Greece the world was alive with spiritual presences, from Zeus, father of the gods, to the naiades, dryads and oreads believed to dwell in rivers, trees and caves. Health, prosperity and abundant offspring, all depended on successfully manipulating these gods and spirits. A handful of intellectuals started to suggest more scientific explanations for the workings of the universe, but most Greeks still put their faith in properly performed sacrifices and other religious rituals.

OF GODS AND MEN

The poets Homer and Hesiod in the 8th century BC created a more orderly pantheon out of

the confused mass of deities inherited from earlier cultures. From the late 5th century BC,

mystery cults, involving secret initiation, flourished around centres such as Eleusis in Attica.

GODS, GODDESSES and other supernatural presences were believed to influence every aspect of life in ancient Greece, residing in magnificent temples or working their magic from beneath the soil. They were associated with local streams, caverns or trees. They exercised their influence over family life from the household hearth; they also arrived in one's dreams to cure, advise or predict. Their intercession was sought at every important juncture in life using a variety of sacrifices, rituals and prayers. If a couple wanted to conceive a boy they would attempt to arrange it with the gods, just as the city-state would seek signs of divine approval before embarking on a war, or a shepherd would seek the gods' help in increasing the size of his flock.

In Greek religion, there was no book of doctrine to tell people how they should worship. As a result, the Greeks were ready to embrace any of various foreign gods and cults that appealed to them. Some had been introduced by far-off ancestors who swept from southern Russia into the Greek peninsula around 3-2000 BC. Others originated in the Minoan civilisation of Crete and the Mycenaean culture centred on the north-eastern Peloponnese. Still others had first exerted their sometimes savage influence in prehistorical times. During the 5th century BC new gods were imported from Thrace and Egypt.

IMPOSING ORDER ON THE GODS

It was the poets Homer and Hesiod in the 8th century BC who imposed order upon the mass of gods and beliefs inherited from earlier times. Stories of divine excesses had reached such a degree, including rape, that Homer, in particular, felt it necessary to sanitise their histories. This was not because the Greeks would have been unduly shocked by such behaviour; it was prompted more by the educated impulse to impose order. So the gods came to be regarded as being appreciative of a finely decorated pot or a well-acted drama performed in their honour. At the same time, in a society that was becoming increasingly

GODS OUT OF DATE
The gods of classical Greece developed from and replaced these earlier deities.

POET GLORIFIED A relief of around 200 BC shows Homer – enthroned, bottom left – receiving the tribute of the gods and muses. Zeus presides at the top.

civilised animal, rather than human, sacrifice was seen as a more acceptable means of placating gods. Even Zeus, the father of the gods, gradually evolved into the upholder of justice rather than the scourge of mortal and divine beings alike.

A family tree of 12 principal gods dwelling on Mount Olympus was the conventionally recognised complement from the 5th century BC onwards, although the fertility god Dionysus and the hero Heracles also attained a degree of Olympian status. It was Homer and Hesiod who gave them their distinct characters and appearances. Because Homer's epic poems were set in the aristocratic society that preceded the democracy of the 5th century BC, his gods behaved like chieftains, solely motivated by their own desires. Although it was important for the gods' own prestige that wrongdoers, mortal or immortal, should be seen to be punished, they had no qualms about lying or dealing unfairly if this was the only means of achieving their ends.

These 'supermen', distinguished from their mortal counterparts by their greater strength, skill and immortality, were just as prone to caprice, bad moods or generous impulses as the Greek warriors themselves. There was no conception of a virtuous life on earth being rewarded after death, and such afterlife as was believed to exist was regarded as shadowy and miserable.

For the Classical Greek Homer was *the* poet – the man who in the *Iliad* and the *Odyssey* gave them the nearest equivalent to the Bible. It was from Homer's epics that rules of religious ritual were derived, as well as precepts for good living – the importance of coming out top in every venture and the maintenance of honour at all costs – which every schoolboy absorbed.

Although by the 6th century BC, and increasingly in the 5th century, a few independently minded men had begun to question some of the more outlandish activities of the gods, explicit atheism was almost unknown. For example, no one could be a good Athenian without believing in the power of the city's patron goddess Athena, and every form of social grouping was also a religious association. The family worshipped at its altar in the courtyard, while worship of common gods, at sanctuaries such as those of Apollo at Delphi and Zeus at Olympia, together with a common language, defined one as being a Greek rather than a barbarian (that is, a foreigner). Gradually, the aristocratic cults of an earlier age were absorbed into a calendar of religious festivals around which the Greeks arranged their lives. It was a corporate, active and festive religion in which introspection had no place.

DUTIES OF PRIESTHOOD

Being a priest was never a full-time job. Priests were responsible for performing all the various rituals prescribed for the site or shrine in their charge, but they had no authority elsewhere. In theory, anybody could

HOMELY SACRIFICE A man pours out a libation (liquid offering) at a household shrine.

WATER BEARERS Men in Athens' annual Panathenaic procession carry pitchers of water for use in sacrifices.

become one since no special qualifications were needed. Often, though, priests were state officials, and in certain cases attributes such as virginity or physical beauty were stipulated.

The priesthood was a prestigious but usually unpaid activity, although most priests could expect to receive perks, such as the skins of sacrificial animals and choice portions of the sacrificial meats. They might also be allotted special seats at the theatre and were sometimes granted honorary wreaths by the state they had served or personal handouts by grateful individuals.

The cult of the gods consisted of purification, sacrifice and prayer. Celebrants purified themselves (usually by washing their hands) before offering the sacrifice, which was seen as a 'favour' extended

by a mortal to the gods. It was intended to put the gods under an obligation to return the favour.

Celebrants stood, with their arms raised up to the sky, when addressing celestial deities, or prostrated themselves on the ground when appealing to the gods of the underworld. First came the invocation of the god or goddess concerned, followed by a reminder of the various pious acts the individual, group or city had performed in the past. Then came the request. In the official prayers of their

ATHENA THE VIRGIN The sculptor Phidias' huge gold and ivory statue of Athena Parthenos (Athena the Virgin) dominates the dimly lit interior of the Parthenon. The only direct light reaching the interior came from the east door.

SEAT OF THE GODS Olympus rises 9570 ft (2917 m) above sea level on the borders of Thessaly and Macedonia.

city, the people of Athens asked the gods, above all Zeus and Athena, to ensure 'the well-being and safety of the citizens of Athens, and of their wives and children, and of the whole country together with her allies'. An individual, on the other hand, might pray: 'Maiden Athena, Telesinos [the name of the person praying] dedicated this image to you on the Acropolis. May you take delight in it, and allow him to dedicate another' – by preserving his life and wealth.

Most people felt some special affinity for a particular god, making different offerings according to their means and the importance of their requests. They had no qualms about informing a god or goddess that if he or she could see a way of making them more prosperous, they would be able to bring larger offerings in future. In any case, the gods were entitled to a share of all human produce – a share of the harvest, libations (when olive oil or wine was poured on the ground), the spoils of war, beautiful pots, cakes or pastries, all of which were left at the site to decompose or be eaten by animals.

The most important of all the sacrifices were blood offerings. Only the very rich could afford to make these at home. The poor had to make do with public sacrifices – one of the rare occasions when they would eat meat. Rams, ewes, cows, oxen, pigs, goats and deer were all slaughtered for this purpose. Each deity had his or her particular preference: Poseidon favoured bulls; Athena, cows; Artemis and Aphrodite were partial to goats. The animals were ideally healthy and without blemish, and their sex and colour were also important: goddesses normally had female animals sacrificed to them; the celestial deities preferred white beasts; while the gods of the underworld preferred dark-skinned offerings.

As the sun rose, the sacrificial victim – garlanded with leaves, woollen ribbons and sometimes with gilded horns – was led to an altar covered with flowers and leaves. The priest and his assistants, who were wreathed and dressed in white, sprinkled themselves and the animal with holy water and lit a fire on the altar. They threw a few grains of barley into the fire, along with some hair clipped from the animal's head. After a prayer, the priest pulled back the victim's head and slit its throat with a single stroke. The blood was meant to spatter the altar, after which the thigh bones were wrapped in fat and burnt in honour of the god. The remaining meat was roasted and divided among the people, who either consumed it then and there or else took it home to eat later. Alternatively, the whole animal might be incinerated as a 'holocaust' – from the words *holos*, 'whole', and *kaio*, 'I burn'. Holocausts were often used for special purificatory sacrifices.

Like all ancient peoples, the Greeks believed that certain conditions or objects were 'unclean', bringing ritual defilement to people who had contact with them.

THE SUPREME A bronze head of Zeus from the 5th century BC gives him suitably stern and regal features.

Anything connected with birth or death was considered unclean. Contact with, say, a dead body thus brought defilement which could be removed only by special purificatory rites. On a more mundane level, you had to expiate on the spot any impious word spoken, if only by spitting.

GODS OF THE UNDERWORLD

In contrast to the gods of Olympus, a different subculture of older deities existed beneath the soil. The underworld was the province of Zeus' brother Hades, who stood guardian over hosts of vaguely conceived ghosts existing unhappily and perpetually within its confines – also known as Hades.

Gathered around the god Hades was yet another group of heroes and earth gods, known as *chthonioi*, who had some local influence over the growth of crops and the souls of the dead. Chthonic gods were worshipped in underground caves – as opposed to the temples dedicated to the Olympian gods – and at night, rather than during the day. In the *Argonautica*, written by the poet Apollonius of Rhodes in the 3rd century BC, the sorcerer-princess Medea advises the hero Jason to dress in sombre clothes and to sacrifice a lamb in a well-rounded pit before praying to Hekate, a goddess of the underworld, and giving her a libation of honey: 'When thou hast thus mindfully propitiated the goddess, get thee away back from the pyre; and let neither thud of feet nor howl of dogs tempt thee to look back, lest thou bring all to nought and thyself return not to thy comrades in seemly wise.'

Very often, warrior heroes such as those of Homer's epics were also worshipped as minor deities. A city might found a hero-cult to solicit a hero's beneficent influence or to appease the spirit of a neglected hero who was believed to be punishing the local people with plague or some other horror. Heracles was the greatest of these heroes. His courage, strength and mythical exploits propelled him into the company of the Olympians – the only hero to achieve immortality.

Another cast of characters above ground included Pan (who looked after flocks of goats and sheep) and the nymphs who were particularly popular with the peasants. These rural deities populated rivers and streams (the nymphs who presided over these were known as naiades), forests and trees (dryads) and mountains and caves (oreads), making the crops grow, and teasing other beings who dwelt nearby. If, for example, the nymph Echo picked up Pan's pipes in the wild, there was no knowing what could happen: the flocks might be sent into a stampede – hence the word 'panic'. An insulted nymph was even thought capable of sending a man insane. More helpfully for humans, the nymph Eileithyia assisted women in childbirth. There were also sea nymphs (oceanids) and other nature spirits, such as the woodland satyrs (with goat-like legs, ears and short horns) and the centaurs, half-horse and half-man and renowned for their lawless behaviour.

More radical religious beliefs included that of Pythagoras the mathematician who taught that souls migrated after death into other bodies, both

continued on page 137

LUSTY GODS Boreas, god of the north wind, carries off Oreithyia, daughter of a legendary king of Athens.

THE DIVINE FAMILY TREE

The Greeks' chief gods and goddesses formed an often quarrelsome family living on the rocky summit of Mount Olympus.

THE HEAD of the divine family was Zeus, whose own father Cronos, king of an earlier family of gods, the Titans, was warned that one of his offspring would dethrone him. To try to prevent this, he swallowed each child as it was born. Zeus, however, escaped this fate when his mother Rhea wrapped a stone in swaddling bands and gave that to her husband instead. He grew up hidden in a cave on Crete and when he reached manhood fulfilled the prophecy by leading a successful rebellion against Cronos and the Titans.

HERA The goddess of marriage was a jealous, volatile character, not much liked by the Greeks. She was Zeus' sister and his only legitimate wife. Hera was a manipulative figure in a difficult marriage riven with quarrels.

ARES Although formerly the god of war, Ares had been demoted to a troublesome and irritating figure by the 5th century BC.

HEPHAESTUS The lame god of fire and metalworking was regarded as the divine smith and the patron of craftsmen.

APHRODITE The goddess of love and female beauty was married to the ugliest immortal, Hephaestus. Aphrodite was also the only one of all the goddesses to commit adultery.

ARTEMIS Originally the mother of all living things, Artemis was the goddess of hunters. She also presided over childbirth.

POSEIDON Zeus' brother was god of the sea and protector of Corinth. Greek fishermen appealed to him when the waves rose around their fragile boats.

ZEUS In arid Greece, Zeus' charge of the weather was a crucial role. To the farmer it was never just 'raining' – instead he gratefully acknowledged that 'Zeus sends the rain'. Terrifying paterfamilias that he was – the thunderbolt and eagle were his emblems – Zeus was still susceptible to the machinations of the other gods.

HESTIA Zeus' sister, the goddess of the hearth, watched over family life.

DEMETER Goddess of agriculture, grain and the harvest, Demeter was closely associated with cereal crops. She was also mother of Persephone – Zeus was the father – famous for her abduction by Hades, King of Underworld.

HERMES Resourceful Hermes was the god of Arcadian shepherds and of travellers everywhere. He was the messenger of the gods and also conducted souls to Hades. His customary garb consisted of sandals, staff and wide-brimmed traveller's hat.

APOLLO With his bow, music, love of beauty and moderating counsel, Apollo embodied that Hellenic spirit. He was always depicted as a beautiful youth, full of athletic grace.

ATHENA The virgin warrior Athena was born fully grown from the head of Zeus. Majestic and serene, she was the patroness of handicrafts, particularly spinning and weaving. She was the household god of Mycenaean palaces and evolved her warlike mien from that belligerent society.

DIONYSUS Greek myth gave Dionysus a double birth, once from a mortal mother, Semele, and again from Zeus' thigh. This gave him a double nature, reflected in his role as god of both joy and madness, and hence of wine. He was the god of the theatre.

ANATOMY OF A GREEK TEMPLE

IN THE TRADITIONAL Homeric view of religion, the gods spent most of their time on Mount Olympus, but they visited their temples in person to receive the offerings of mortals. A typical sanctuary was surrounded by a wall with an open court, the temple itself and an altar outside it. The area was sometimes in an isolated place and might enclose a mountain top, a grove of trees, a strangely shaped rock, or a cave. Varying rules were laid down for those entering sanctified land. In one instance, shoes made of pigskin were banned; in another, all beasts of burden were barred; in a third, lighting a fire in the precinct would incur a fine of 10 drachmas.

Carved garlands, bulls' heads and other decorations sometimes festooned temples. The altars – upright stone structures – were positioned at the front of the temple in the sanctuary courtyard. The people congregated around the temple and worshipped in the open air. The larger temples frequently had stepped altars, whose size could vary from just over 630 ft (190 m) long – as in the largest known altar at Syracuse – to a modest 16 ft 6 in (5 m).

Temples gradually evolved from small, rectangular buildings with a single cell-like room, mud-brick walls, thatched roof and a simple porch, to more elaborate wooden structures, some of whose features were later translated into stone. These earlier temples often had a room at the back for the priest and the storage of temple treasures. Stone-built temples began to appear around 700 BC.

The crowning glory of Athens's Acropolis, the Parthenon, was finished during the age of the great statesman Pericles in the 5th century. It contained a 40 ft (12 m) high, ivory and gold statue of the goddess Athena, to whom it was dedicated. The temple also included some sophisticated optical refinements. The outside columns were

POSTURE OF PRAYER A bronze statuette from around 500 BC shows a Greek worshipper with his arms raised as he implores the favour of the gods.

built leaning in slightly, so that their centrelines, if they were extended upwards, would converge a mile (1.6 km) above the earth's surface – this offset the illusion that the columns are leaning outwards normally created by perimeter columns. Similarly, the horizontal base on which the temple columns stand was built with a slight curve, so that it is higher at the centre than the ends, counteracting the illusion of sagging. Another refinement was in the sculpted figures decorating the frieze at eaves' level. The carved figures are, in fact, distorted, but appear normal when seen by spectators at ground level.

RUINED GLORY   Remains at Segesta in Sicily bear testimony to the perfect proportions of Greek temple-building.

FOR SACRIFICE   A procession of women, bearing branches and playing pipes and a lyre, leads a sheep to the altar.

human and animal. Meat-eating was therefore taboo, as it was for the Orphics – followers of the mythical singer Orpheus. The Orphics believed that the body was a prison for the soul. After death, the souls of Orphic initiates were believed to live in happiness; the souls of non-initiates were purified in the under-world. Both Orphic and Pythagorean creeds were too intellectual and dogmatic, however, to be widely adopted by ordinary people.

REVELS WITH THE GOD OF FERTILITY

Spectacular as it was, the religion bequeathed by Homer was coldly utilitarian. For the common man, Dionysus, the fertility god, held more appeal, since worshipping him involved wild dancing and drinking, building up to a kind of spiritual ecstasy. This form of 'possession' offered temporary release from the self and kinship with a god. Although Dionysus was never accorded fully equal status with the Olympian family, he had his own temple on the slopes of the Acropolis and a part share in Apollo's shrine at Delphi. He was also worshipped in the towns or fields in the spring, and with twice-yearly festivals on the mountain tops in winter. Women, in particular, the most restricted social group apart from slaves, found the possibility of release in night-time Dionysiac ecstasy appealing.

A vivid account comes from Euripides' play *The Bacchae*, in which the women of Thebes become possessed by Dionysus who 'pricks them to leave their looms and shuttles'. Dressed in deerskins and carrying staves garlanded with ivy and vine leaves, they dance to a remote mountain place in proces-sion headed by a long-haired effeminate priest, who is in fact the god himself. Here, as the smoke rises from their torches, the crowd, draped with snakes, dances to the heartbeat of the tympanum – a drum made from a circle of stretched hide. Piercing the air are the thin notes of the reed-flute played in ac-companiment, as well as the increasingly frenzied shouts of the crowd. A watching herdsman, mean-while, witnesses visions of the earth erupting with milk, wine and honey. In his vision, it is revealed to him that the participants are endowed with a god-given strength that enables them to tear wild animals to pieces and to eat their raw flesh.

It is not known when the Dionysiac cult, which originated in Asia, infiltrated Greece. But the terri-fying stories circulated by writers such as Plutarch reveal how much it was feared by many educated Hellenes and how fiercely they resisted it. Every-thing about the cult – from the notion of divine possession of mortals to the hysteria it generated – was anathema to many members of a race that was proud of its sanity, moderation and self-possession, unlike the barbaric races surrounding it.

In the event, however, it proved unstoppable among less educated people. With characteristic

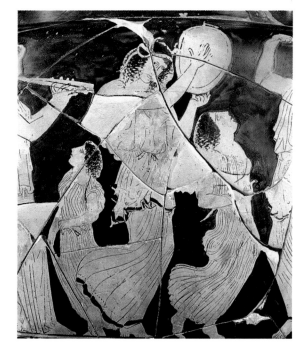

SELF-ABANDON Music and dance set the beat for female cult members during a Dionysiac revel.

pragmatism, those in authority tried to control it by official sanction, eliminating some of its unpalatable aspects. Thus, in winter, it was laid down that Apollo should surrender his place at the great religious centre of Delphi to the young god Dionysus, but that officially chosen maenads – female followers of the god – should direct his festival.

MYSTERIES IN ELEUSIS

Homer's aristocratic gods survived long after the society to which they belonged had disappeared. Athenians continued to battle in the name of Athena – but more because she shared the name of their city than because they were actually going to war in her honour. With the growth of individualism and the simultaneous decline of the city-state at the end of the 5th century BC, the various mystery cults (involving special initiation ceremonies) made a comeback that engulfed the Greek-speaking world.

Most revered of these cults were the Eleusinian mysteries, which honoured Demeter, the Olympian goddess of agriculture, and her daughter Persephone. Rapidly appropriated by Athens – the town of Eleusis was 12 miles (19 km) away – the cult promised some sort of paradise for the dead. As with other mystery cults, entry was by initiation

with candidates invited from all over Greece. The date for the initiation rites was advertised by heralds, sent by two aristocratic families connected with the rite, who proclaimed a holy truce of ten weeks to all the city-states who used the sanctuary.

Men, women and slaves were all eligible to take part in the ceremonies, so long as they were morally fit. About 1000 postulants arrived at Athens for 'The Gathering' – the official opening – having paid a fee equivalent to ten days' wages. Many came from outside Athens and were allocated a personal attendant to help them through the complicated rituals.

The first few days were taken up with purificatory rites and sacrifices. The fourth day began on a sombre note as the participants were confined indoors – a strange experience for the Greek male – in preparation for the procession to Eleusis on the following day. In strict hierarchical order, and accompanied by elaborately dressed priests and a military escort, the crowd set off, adorned with garlands and carrying branches of myrtle and sometimes bags of provisions. Most walked, perhaps with a donkey or mule to carry their baggage, to the accompaniment of the flautists, harp players and choristers who punctuated their ranks. They would stop regularly to worship at sacred sites, and at one point they would even be waylaid by men with covered heads who hurled abuse at them from a bridge – a means of frightening off evil spirits. Finally, the torchlit procession arrived at Eleusis and the rest of the night was spent singing and dancing in honour of the Eleusinian goddesses. Huge offerings of corn were made to Demeter – on one occasion, enough to feed 1000 men for a day. There was fasting, sacrifices and a display of the sacred objects in the Telesterion – that is, the Hall of Mysteries, lit by a skylight in the centre of the roof.

The central rite was a closely guarded secret, but it probably retold the myth of Demeter whose

EYES OF A GOD Dionysus' eyes on a drinking vessel were said to ward off evil spirits while you drank.

MUSIC FROM THE MUSES

The word 'music' comes from the nine Muses, the daughters of Zeus and Mnemosyne, goddess of memory. Each had responsibility for an art or science. Calliope was usually regarded as the patron of epic poetry, Clio of history, Erato of love poetry, Euterpe of flute-playing, Melpomene of lyre-playing, Polyhymnia of geometry, Terpsichore of dancing, Thalia of comedy and Urania of astonomy.

daughter Persephone was abducted by Hades. Demeter in her sorrow would not let crops grow, until Zeus bargained with Hades to let Persephone come up to the upper world. Unfortunately, this release was only partial, because Persephone had eaten the seeds of a pomegranate during her abduction. This act of eating, symbolic for the Greeks of marriage, kept her partially bound to the underworld, so that she was only free to return to the upper world for six months of each year. Her mother Demeter was happy when Persephone was in the world and crops accordingly grew; she was sad when Persephone returned to the underworld and crops died back. As it was Demeter who brought life to the dead ground, so she was believed to offer hope of life after death to initiates.

OMENS, ORACLES AND SUPERSTITION

Muddled into this range of practices was a further plethora of superstitious beliefs. For example, the birth of a deformed child was considered to be a formidable 'sign' of the gods' disapproval. Zeus was thought to speak through the rain and thunder. Any unexpected encounter or sound, particularly in the morning, was either a good or an unlucky omen depending on whether it came from the left-hand side or the right – the right was lucky.

Educated people like the statesman-general Nicias (c.470-413 BC) surrounded themselves with diviners and oracle-mongers and responded to strange events with as much superstitious conviction as the man in the fields. The dependable Nicias lost an army and was killed in Sicily because an eclipse of the moon made him delay a crucial withdrawal. On hearing the news, no Athenian would have doubted the general's courage or impugned

DIONYSIAC FUN A satyr is entwined with vine branches on a bronze vessel found in a grave in northern Greece.

SPEAKING APOLLO'S WORD Delphi, on the slopes of Mount Parnassus, was the home of the most famous of Greek oracles. Its mouthpiece was the Pythia, a woman always over 50 years old and living apart from her husband.

MORE CHILDREN, PLEASE This plaque was found at Dodona in north-western Greece, home of an oracle of Zeus. In it a man called Hermon asks 'to which god he should pray to have useful children by his wife, Eretaia, apart from those he already has'.

his judgment in reacting to such an obviously divine sign. His mistake, they would have said, lay in consulting the wrong seer who misinterpreted the eclipse: Nicias should have known that when an army wished to retreat, an eclipse of the moon was a favourable portent. However, the superstition was not universal: the historian Thucydides blamed Nicias for being 'overfond of divination'.

The most highly regarded form of all divination was oracular prophecy, in which professional seers went into a trance to reveal the will of a god. A sceptical writer of the 2nd century BC gave an irreverent account of a day in the life of one overworked god: 'Apollo now finds himself practically deafened by importunate bores who come and clamour for oracles everywhere . . . Whenever a prophetess (having swigged her sacred water, chewed up some laurel leaves, and wriggled about on the tripod for a bit) invokes his presence, he must rush straight off and mug up the right oracles, or else ruin all his carefully built-up professional prestige.'

Delphi, with its temple of Apollo, is the best known of the oracular sites that dotted Greece – an evocative place, situated high above a gorge and surmounted by imposing rose-coloured precipices. Originally, the oracle at Delphi was only consulted by the leaders of a group of mainland states, but by the 5th century BC it was inspiring wider respect. Once a month, but never during the winter, men travelled from all over the Greek world to visit the Pythia – a specialist priestess. After all those involved, including the Pythia, had purified themselves, a priest presented a goat to Apollo. If the animal trembled, the day was considered auspicious and the beast sacrificed. In fact, the chances of the day being other than auspicious were small, since the goat was sprinkled with water to encourage it to shiver – only a failure to shiver would render the day inauspicious. That ritual accomplished, the inquirers presented their questions to the Pythia through the priests who interpreted her answers, often in verse and, on request, in writing.

Most historians believe that the seer's trance was genuine and that the pronouncements were given in good faith. Fortunately, they were open to wide interpretation. When the Athenians, faced with an invasion by the Persians in 479 BC, consulted Apollo at Delphi, they were told to 'trust in the wooden walls'. A few thought this referred to the wooden defences on the top of the Acropolis, but these were captured by the invaders. Apollo's meaning became clear when the Greeks defeated the Persians in the naval battle of Salamis in 480 BC – by 'wooden walls', Apollo had meant ships.

Most of the oracles' business was on a private level – often proposals for which the oracle had only to answer in the affirmative. For example, 'Lysanias asks . . . whether the child Annyla is pregnant with, is his'; 'Cleotas asks whether it would be beneficial and advantageous for him to keep sheep'; 'Agis asks . . . about the blankets and pillows which he has lost. Could they have been taken by an outside burglar?' Everyone consulted oracles – rich, poor, free or slave. 'Is my escape to be intercepted?' asks one. 'Shall I receive the money?' and 'Shall I be ambassador?' ask others. The accuracy or otherwise of the answers is not often recorded.

WISE ADVICE Aegeus, legendary King of Athens, consults the oracle of Themis, goddess of wisdom.

SCIENCE AND MEDICINE

Healing practices based on religion and superstition existed alongside the new

methods of the Hippocratic school which ascribed sickness to physical causes.

Natural scientists, meanwhile, were bandying around some eccentric theories about the world.

GREEK PHYSICIANS can be said to have invented modern medicine, though their teachings rarely filtered down to the ordinary people of their time. Figures such as Hippocrates – living from about 469 to 370 BC and remembered to this day in the Hippocratic oath sworn by doctors – were among the first to announce that sickness and healing had physical causes, rather than being simply a result of the activities of the gods or magical spells. It was a revolutionary way of looking at things – which in

practice had little effect on the methods used by most ordinary people to deal with illness. For them, the role of the supernatural remained supreme.

Healing gods and heroes had abounded in Greece for centuries, most notably Asclepius, revered first as a hero and later as a god. According to mythology, he was the son of Apollo by the nymph Coronis and was taught the healing arts by the centaur Chiron. Shrines dedicated to him were littered with miniature models of injured limbs or sick organs (rather like those seen in some Catholic

HEALING DREAM The mythical hero Amphiaraus of Thebes appears to a sleeping invalid in this 4th-century BC relief. Amphiaraus was one of a number of heroes and minor divinities believed to have the healing touch.

THE YEARS OF ATHENS' GREAT PLAGUE

AS DAWN BROKE on a spring day in 431 BC, soldiers who had been on lookout duty through the night rushed down from the towers on Athens' city walls with alarming news: the Spartan army had arrived on the plain below. The news was greeted with terror and dismay by citizens whose numbers had been swollen by an influx of country-dwellers seeking protection in the city. These people had dispatched their livestock to the island of Euboea off Attica for safer keeping, and now looked out in particular horror to see their farms being torched by the Spartans; the smoke of burning crops and olive trees hung in a viscous pall over the enemy's route as they crossed the plain.

Inside the city, every inch of space was taken up by the refugees; some were even camping in the area that lay between the Long Walls. During the course of the following year, as the Spartan siege prolonged itself, huts mushroomed along the Long Walls all the way to the harbour, while inside the walls, people lived like animals wherever they could find a space to put up a few boards and a roof of hide. Some even had recourse to cooking and sleeping in the shrines or in the colonnades of the wrestling schools.

By the spring of 430, as the returning heat revitalised the stinking pools of refuse and excrement, plague broke out. The sickness began with hoarseness, bleeding at the throat and then progressed to convulsions and violent internal pains. People's skin assumed a liverish colour and was covered in supurating sores, making clothing unbearable to wear; the only thing sick people yearned to do was to throw themselves into cold water. Death came on the seventh or eighth day, and took the statesman Pericles among many hundreds of others. A few people, including the historian Thucydides, were lucky enough to survive the sickness – and were immune from the plague from that time onwards.

For all of that year and well into the next, the plague raged on, dispatching a quarter of the entire population of Athens to Hades below. With life so uncertain, lawlessness and blasphemous behaviour were the order of the day. The dead were cremated in untidy heaps (when the Spartans understood the meaning of those plumes of smoke they immediately withdrew from Attica) and some people even had recourse to hijacking funeral pyres in their desperation to dispose of their relations. 'They would anticipate the builders of a pyre, put their own dead on it and set it alight, or throw the corpse they were carrying on top of an already lighted pyre and leave it', observed Thucydides. He also noted that self-gratification had become the normal way of behaving for citizens whose lives and wealth 'were liable to perish at any moment'.

shrines today). The shrines generally stood by healing springs; some had dining rooms, recreational courtyards, theatres and stone beds for the 'sleep' cure. For this patients spent a night in the shrine's temple. As they slept, it was believed that the god of the shrine would visit them and either cure them on the spot or prescribe treatment.

The most famous healing centre was Epidaurus in the north-eastern Peloponnese, which claimed several extraordinary cures, including the supposed filling of an empty socket with a new eye. In another case, the healing god was supposed to have delivered a child to a woman who had been pregnant with it for five years. As various cautionary tales illustrate, it was never worth risking the displeasure of such gods. A blind man who refused to pay when his sight was restored lost his sight again. Another story tells of a man who had been cured of facial scars. He sent his fee through a friend who kept the money – only to find that he, himself, was now similarly afflicted. When the

ΑCΚΛΗ
ΠΙΩ
ΚΑΙ
ΫΓΕΙΑ
ΤΥΧΗ
ΕΥΧΑΡΙC
ΤΗΡΙΟΝ

TYCHE'S THANKS A patient named Tyche whose leg had healed left this token of gratitude to Asclepius.

thief asked to be cured, the god took the first man's bandage and laid it on his face – with the result that he was immediately burdened with his friend's former scars as well as his own.

Although magic – the use of spells, rather than prayers to the gods, to bring about changes – was of only marginal importance in Greek daily life, it was certainly practised. Magical practices appear in Homer's *Odyssey*, and the witches of Thessaly in central Greece, who were deemed responsible for 'calling down the moon' when there was an eclipse, were famous from about 500 BC onwards. Plato criticised various witch doctors for leeching the rich with promises of bringing them health and happy lives through magic incantations.

In marked contrast were the rational medical treatises that members of Hippocrates' school were writing on the island of Cos from the late 5th century BC onwards. Hippocrates himself is a somewhat shadowy figure about whom little is known for sure. He was famous enough to be mentioned by Plato and Aristotle in their works, and seems to have travelled widely throughout the Greek world, teaching and practising his medical skills.

The medical school on Cos commonly associated with him was probably his base. The revolutionary approach he and his pupils espoused is well summed up in their attitude to epilepsy usually then believed to be a divine punishment. 'The

DOCTOR'S EXAMINATION The tomb of the 2nd-century BC physician, Jason, shows him examining a boy.

so-called sacred disease is due to the same causes as all other diseases, to bodily intake and waste, to cold and sun and constant atmosphere and weather changes,' Hippocrates wrote staunchly.

Some of the cures attributed to Hippocrates focused on restoring the right equilibrium to the four humours – blood, phlegm, choler and bile – of which the body was thought to be composed. This was achieved by dieting, purging, blood-letting

A DOCTOR'S LOYALTY TO HIS TEACHER

THE HIPPOCRATIC OATH – almost certainly not composed by Hippocrates, though enshrining many of his values – placed as much stress on the young doctor's obligations to his fraternity as on healing the sick. He promised:

❛ To regard my teacher in this art as equal to my parents; to make him partner in my livelihood, and when he is in need of money to share mine with him; to consider his offspring equal to my brothers;

to teach them this art, if they require to learn it, without fee or indenture; and to impart precept, oral instruction, and all other learning to my sons to the sons of my teacher, and to pupils who have signed the indenture and sworn obedience to the Physicians' Law, but to none other. ❜

PIONEER PHYSICIAN Hippocrates laid the foundations for the scientific study of medicine.

FROM TROY TO ALEXANDER The Homeric hero Achilles (right) binds the wounds of his friend Patroclus – war wounds were a common source of injuries among the belligerent Greek states. Surgical instruments (above) from the period after Alexander the Great's death in 323 BC bear witness to advances in the arts of healing.

and surgery. Here, the Hippocratic doctors were mistaken, as they were when it came to anatomy which they could only study through operations and by dissecting animals, since human post-mortems were taboo. Of lasting significance, however, was their role as the first people to study the developing symptoms of the patient so that they could predict the course of a specific illness.

THE ART OF ASKING QUESTIONS

This habit of questioning the world about them – of not being content with traditional answers and wanting to learn more – gave rise to some of the ancient Greeks' greatest achievements in many fields of knowledge. On the other hand, this form

of intellectual enquiry was always restricted to a handful of highly educated people. The person in the street was automatically distrustful of anyone who questioned any of the traditional assumptions on which the social order was supposed to be based. Happily he was mostly unaware of such activities and only brayed for blood when supposed blasphemy was pushed under his nose, as when Socrates was made a scapegoat for Athens' political turmoil around the turn of the 5th and 4th centuries BC by being publicly denounced for irreligion.

PERFECT PROPORTIONS   Science and art met in a fascination with proportion, especially in the human body.

The scientific revolution had begun in the 6th century BC in the Ionian Greek cities on the coast of Asia Minor and, among the educated, generated the same excited controversy that Darwin and Freud's writings did in more recent times.

The first notable figure was Thales of Miletus, said to have introduced geometry to Greece from Egypt. He also came up with the theory that water was the primary activator in the world. Earthquakes happened, according to him, when the water on which the earth rested was made turbulent by wind. He was not right, of course, but it was significant that he did not attribute such natural catastrophes to the gods.

Other early thinkers put forward an 'atomic' theory of the universe, proposing that matter consisted of tiny particles invisible to the human eye which did not change but regrouped in different formations to make up the visible world.

Arguments like these were batted back and forth among intellectuals, but beyond the atomic theory, few scientific truths were discovered because none of the assumptions made were put to the proof. Educated Greeks had a distaste for the workaday mechanics of technology; they also believed that existence was rational and that sheer hard thought was all that was needed to understand it. So their guesses remained guesses, logically argued from a close observation of the world but never tested by experiment.

Sometimes their 'truths' were derived from an analogy with human institutions. One philosopher, Anaximandros, described the mechanics of the universe as a balancing act performed by opposing elements 'paying the penalty and recompensing one another for their injustice' just as happened in human law courts. He also took a leap from received opinion, as well as chancing upon a truth, when he declared that the earth was an unsupported and small body in relation to the cosmos.

WHO ARE THE GODS?

The educated minority debated everything: the nature of justice, of right and wrong, of power and the belief that might is right. While some such as the 6th-century BC mathematician and philosopher Pythagoras sounded the depths of mysticism, others explored in a different direction, asking if the traditional gods were just a social convention.

One religious thinker was the poet and philosopher Xenophanes – probably born around 570 BC at Colophon on the coast of modern Turkey but spending much of his life in the Greek city of Elea in southern Italy. As he observed: 'The Ethiopians say that their gods are snub-nosed and black; and the Thracians, that theirs are blue-eyed and red-haired.' If different peoples known to the Greeks had no uniform idea of what their gods looked like, was it possible that the gods were different in other ways, too, from what people had traditionally believed about them? He even proposed that there was one god only, who was 'not like mortals either in body or in mind'.

He went on to attack Homer and Hesiod for attributing to the gods all the things 'that among men earn shame and abuse – theft, adultery and

THE GREAT MATHEMATICIANS

THE GREEK CITIES of southern Italy and Sicily were vibrant hubs of intellectual activity, presided over by figures such as Hieron I, tyrant of Syracuse in Sicily from 478 to 466 BC and a generous patron of the arts, though despotic in politics. Equally notable were the cities associations with two of the most famous of Greek mathematicians, Pythagoras and Archimedes.

Pythagoras was born around 580 BC on Samos, but spent most of his adult life in Croton (modern Crotóne) in Calabria. As a mathematician he was the first to classify numbers as odd, even, prime and so forth. He also discovered the mathematical basis of musical notation, as well as his famous theorem about the squares on the sides of a triangle. But his speculations ranged more widely than that. An impressive figure, in gold coronet, white robe and trousers, he was a philosopher and priest rolled into one, founding a religious movement whose beliefs were only to be revealed to initiates. He believed that the soul was a fallen divinity confined within the body as a tomb and condemned to a cycle of reincarnation. It could be released by cultivating piety. His beliefs were to

STUDY SHEET This papyrus fragment comes from a geometry textbook.

DEATH OF A GENIUS A mosaic shows Archimedes' death at the hands of a Roman soldier. His home city Syracuse was a famous centre of learning.

influence Plato, Aristotle and many later philosophers.

Born in Syracuse around 287 BC, Archimedes studied at Alexandria, the great centre of learning founded by Alexander the Great. Back in Syracuse, he invented the waterscrew and various engines of war, all of which were put to use when his city was besieged by the Romans, a growing power in Italy. He discovered the principle of the lever – giving rise to the saying attributed to him: 'Give me a place to stand on and I will move the earth.' Most famously, he discovered the

principle of buoyancy, supposedly when he noticed the amount of water his body displaced in the bath. In his excitement after this discovery he is said to have run naked through the streets shouting '*Eureka!*' ('I have found it!').

His death came at the hands of the Romans. In 212 Syracuse fell to the Roman general Marcellus. He gave orders that the great mathematician should be spared, but in the widespread slaughter a soldier stabbed Archimedes, apparently while he was drawing a geometrical figure in the sand with his finger.

THEORIES ABOUT THE UNIVERSE

THE SEAPORT of Miletus, on the west coast of modern Turkey, was famous in the 6th century BC as one of the foremost centres of learning in the Greek world. In that century it produced three of the pioneers of Greek philosophy, Thales, Anaximander and Anaximenes, whose discourses were subsequently written down in some of the earliest Greek books. Each held interesting ideas about the universe.

Anaximander believed that the world and many other worlds invisible to mortals were surrounded and suspended within an undefined 'Boundless'. Around the tub-shaped earth were great rings of fire – the sun, moon and stars – each concealed in tubes of mist with holes in it through which the inferno blazed out. Anaximenes held that the earth was surrounded by air and was flat and thin – like a pizza base in modern terms. Mists rose from the earth and changed into blazing leaf shapes making the sun, stars and the moon. Eclipses occurred when other solid bodies moved in front of them.

The Milesians were unable to divorce themselves entirely from the assumptions of the myth-makers who had gone before them. They retained the idea that the sky existed at a fixed distance from the earth, and generally believed (with the exception of Anaximander) that some sort of material supported the earth from below. They all believed that the world was as it was seen, and that although human senses were too weak to grasp all, a close observation of the visible enabled conclusions about the world beyond perception. They made some advances in astronomy – in particular with their conclusion in 500 that the moon gives off reflected light and by the identification of most of the planets by 400.

mutual deceit'. In doing so, in some people's eyes, he was striking a blow at values and precepts for living that underlay the entire society.

THE FATHERS OF HISTORY

The study of history really begins with Herodotus and his account of the Persian war. Born around 484 BC, probably at Halicarnassus (now Bodrum)

LASTING APPEAL   Despite the doubts of intellectuals, the rites of the Eleusinian mysteries kept their appeal.

on modern Turkey's west coast, Herodotus was an unusually well-travelled man. He spent several years living on Samos, visited the Black Sea, Athens and Egypt and died around 425 in the Athenian colony of Thurii in southern Italy. When he was growing up there, Halicarnassus was part of the Persian Empire, so he also had first-hand experience of Persian ways.

His history is far more than a work of military history because he described all the known world. He detailed the geography, tribal customs and important buildings of each nation. In the process, he juxtaposed Grecian democracy with Oriental despotism, showing a fascination, unusual for a Greek, with foreign ways.

By modern standards he was no historian at all. Because he was writing about events that had occurred 50 years before his time and about which there was no documentary evidence, his chronology is eccentric in the extreme. He based his account on conversations with survivors of the Persian wars or even their sons. Consequently, a lot is apocryphal or vague. Sometimes, when faced with two contradictory accounts he presents both without judging between them. Elsewhere, he announces that one version is more probable than others but

LEGACY OF GREECE Phidias and his Parthenon frieze are imagined by the Victorian artist Lawrence Alma-Tadema.

does not explain why. On one occasion he confounds the modern reader by remarking: 'I am obliged to tell what is told, but to believe it I am not entirely obliged, and that is to be taken as holding good for everything which I tell.'

But he was the first to see that the past happened because of the activities of men rather than because of divine manipulation of human puppets. The way he tells the story is like first-rate journalism: racy, stuffed with anecdotes and digressions – from the Egyptians to the Babylonians – and with a keen eye for the dramatic or moving moment.

The Athenian Thucydides, who died around 400 BC, was the first critical historian, producing drier accounts. He dismissed the poets as reliable sources because 'they elaborate and exaggerate' and took a scarcely veiled swipe at Herodotus when he disparaged prose writers who 'prefer the entertainment of their readers to the truth; their facts cannot be checked because of the passage of time and are legend rather than reliable history. My own narrative is based . . . not on a casual enquiry nor on my personal opinion, but partly by following up as closely as I could the accounts of eyewitnesses.'

TIME CHART

2000 – 901 BC

AMONG THE GREEKS

MINOAN AXE Priests used double-headed axes to slaughter bulls.

2000 The Minoans of Crete are reaching the peak of their power and influence. Their civilisation is based on royal palaces, each forming the core of a thriving community.

1400-1200 The Mycenaean culture, centred at Mycenae, Pylos and other sites in the Peloponnese, becomes the dominant power on the Greek mainland. Mycenaeans also arrive in Crete.

1450 A volcano on the island of Thera, 70 miles (110 km) north of Crete, erupts. The eruption probably destroys Knossos and other centres of Crete's Minoan civilisation.

1200 Troy is destroyed as part of a raid or war, probably the basis for Homer's account of the Trojan War.

TROJAN HORSE The real Troy was a rich agricultural centre.

1200 Mycenae and other centres of the Mycenaean culture are burned by unknown raiders – possibly Dorians from northern Greece. This marks the beginning of the culture's decline, ushering in ancient Greece's Dark Ages.

Athens, still a relatively minor settlement, escapes the general destruction. It is well protected by massive walls possibly built after the 12 towns of Attica were united under the rule of the kings of Athens.

1000 The Dorians are well established in the Peloponnese. Greeks from the mainland set out across the Aegean to colonise the coast of Asia Minor.

LIFE AND LEARNING

1900 Young Minoan women and men indulge in the dangerous practice of bull-leaping – possibly a religious rite.

1600-1400 The Palace of Minos at Knossos on Crete is equipped with air and light shafts as well as plumbed bathrooms.

The Minoans use a script known to modern scholars as Linear A for writing on clay tablets. It includes some symbols for whole words, but others representing syllables – allowing words to be built up or spelt.

BULL JUMPERS They grasp the bull's horns and swing themselves onto its back.

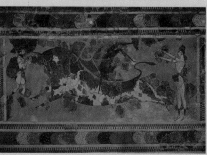

1400-1200 The Mycenaean script Linear B is in use in the Peloponnese and also on Crete. It falls out of use after the collapse of the Mycenaean civilisation around 1200 BC.

The Mycenaeans use light spoke-wheeled, horse-drawn chariots for warfare, hunting and possibly

COLUMNS AT KNOSSOS The royal palace reflected a flourishing civilisation.

travelling. They build some roads that are suitable for wheeled vehicles with bridges to carry them over streams.

800 After a period in which the Greeks seem to have been illiterate, the alphabet of Classical (and modern) Greece develops. It is based on models from Phoenicia and the Near East.

THE REST OF THE WORLD

1750 Babylon is the dominant power in Mesopotamia. Its King Hammurabi will be remembered for collating his people's laws and those of earlier civilisations in the 'Code of Hammurabi'.

1304 In Egypt, Ramses II becomes pharaoh. His 67-year reign will be the second longest in Egyptian history, notable for its prosperity and many building projects. Ramses II is also probably the pharaoh associated with the Jewish exodus under Moses.

1250 The Assyrian Empire is now the dominant Mesopotamian power, reaching a height of magnificence under the extravagant Tukulti-ninurta.

1198 Ramses III of Egypt takes on the mysterious Sea Peoples, warlike

DOUGHTY MONARCH Ramses III of Egypt strikes down a foe.

seafarers probably from Asia Minor and the Aegean islands, who have already overthrown the Hittite Empire.

1110 Under Nebuchadnezzar I Babylon re-establishes its dominance in Mesopotamia. This period also sees a flowering of its arts, producing works such as *The Epic of Gilgamesh*, the tale of a Mesopotamian hero.

1050 The Phoenicians, based in cities such as Tyre and Sidon in the eastern Mediterranean, trade as far afield as Tarshish in southern Spain.

1000 King David captures Jerusalem and goes on to make it the capital of a powerful Jewish state. He will be succeeded by his son Solomon, builder of the first temple in Jerusalem.

WOOL CROP
A Spartan king supervises as wool is weighed.

800 Greek merchants establish a trading post at Al-Mina in northern Syria.

735 Settlers from Chalcis on the Greek island of Euboea found the colony of Naxos on Sicily. This is one of the first Greek colonies established around the Mediterranean.

730 The outbreak of the 19-year Messenian War in which Sparta conquers the neighbouring state of Messenia. The Messenians are reduced to the status of serfs, while Sparta is established as a leading military power.

650 Greek city-states, notably Miletus and Megara, start founding colonies on the coasts of the Black Sea and its approaches.

621 In Athens, Draco issues a law code notable for its harshness – punishing even trivial offences with the death penalty.

594 The former Athenian archon (chief magistrate) Solon embarks on a programme of radical legal and economic reform, which includes undoing some of the severity of Draco's code.

FAILED ASSASSIN
Aristogiton tried, but failed, to murder the Athenian tyrant Hippias in 514.

561 Peisistratus seizes power in Athens as tyrant. Apart from two periods in exile, he remains in power until his death in 527, during which time he institutes the festival of the Dionysia with its drama competitions.

508-507 The Athenian Assembly, under the leadership of the aristocrat Cleisthenes, reforms the city's system of government, laying the foundations for democratic rule.

AMONG THE GREEKS

---

776 The first recorded celebration of the Olympic Games.

750 The *Iliad* and the *Odyssey*, the two epic poems traditionally ascribed to Homer, are written during the 8th century BC.

The Boeotian farmer Hesiod writes his long poem on farming, *Works and Days*, and his account of the creation of the world and the genealogy of the gods, the *Theogony*.

600 Around this time, the first Greek coins are minted on the island of Aegina.

GEOMETRIC STYLE
An Attic vase of around 800 BC.

LYRIC CHARM **The female poet Sappho (*c*.612-*c*.580) of Lesbos.**

585 Thales of Miletus accurately predicts an eclipse of the Sun for May 28. Other natives of Miletus, the greatest of the Ionian Greek cities, include the philosophers Anaximander and Anaximenes.

582 The Pythian Games, held at Delphi, are celebrated for the first time.

581 Corinth's Isthmian Games are held for the first time.

573 The Nemean Games are held for the first time, at Nemea in the north-eastern Peloponnese.

534 The poet Thespis wins the prize for tragedy at Athens' City Dionysia festival. He is considered by some as the father of tragedy.

530 Around this time Athenian potters develop the 'red figure' style – black pots with red figures.

LIFE AND LEARNING

---

753 The traditional date for the founding of Rome.

742 In Jerusalem, the prophet Isaiah calls the people of Judah to holiness. He also teaches the coming of the Messiah.

700 The Assyrian Sennacherib embarks on an ambitious rebuilding of his capital Nineveh, including an 80-room royal palace.

612 The Babylonians and Medes sack Nineveh, signalling the collapse of the once-mighty Assyrian Empire.

586 Nebuchadnezzar II of Babylon sacks Jerusalem, deporting its inhabitants – the start of the Jews' Babylonian captivity.

559 Cyrus the Great becomes king of Persia. Over the next 30 years, he will transform his kingdom into a vast empire, conquering Lydia, the realms of the Medes and Babylonia.

551 The Persian prophet Zoroaster dies. His teachings involve the worship of the god of light and goodness Ormazd, who is engaged in never-ending conflict with the spirit of evil Ahriman.

BEAST OF BABYLON **A lion in glazed tiles from Babylon.**

551 The Chinese philosopher Confucius is born.

546 King Croesus of Lydia dies. Under his rule Lydia has become legendarily rich through commerce.

522 Darius, son of a provincial governor, seizes the Persian throne.

521 Gautama Buddha preaches his first sermon in the deer park of the holy city of Benares (now Varanasi).

THE REST OF THE WORLD

SECURITY **Guardian figures for Assyrian royal palaces.**

500 – 451 BC

AMONG THE GREEKS

BY FOOT AND CHARIOT Athenian soldiers set out for war.

490 The Persians, under Darius the Great, attempt a seaborne invasion of Greece but are defeated at Marathon by an Athenian army.

483 The statesman Themistocles starts building up the Athenian fleet, making him an architect of the eventual defeat of the Persians and of Athens' naval supremacy.

480 The Persians, under Xerxes, defeat a Spartan army at Thermopylae and take Athens, burning the city and destroying the Acropolis. The Athenians then destroy the Persian fleet at Salamis.

479 A Greek army, led by the Spartans, defeats the Persians at Plataea, bringing to an end Persian ambitions to conquer Greece.

FAR SIGHTED Themistocles expanded the Athenian navy.

477 The Delian League is formed – an alliance against the Persians of the islands and cities of the north-eastern Aegean and its coasts. It is led by Athens and will effectively become an Athenian empire.

461-446 First Peloponnesian War. Intermittent hostilities between Athens and the members of the Peloponnesian League led by Sparta.

LIFE AND LEARNING

488-487 The practice of ostracism is introduced in Athens as a means of exiling overmighty citizens. The first victim is Hipparchus, though it is not now known what his offence was.

484 The playwright Aeschylus wins his first victory in the drama competition of Athens' City Dionysia festival.

480 The trireme, originally developed by Phoenician seafarers, proves its worth at the Battle of Salamis. It will remain the standard fighting ship through most of the 5th century BC.

476 The Boeotian-born poet Pindar arrives in Sicily. He will write some of his finest odes at the courts of the tyrants of the Greek cities of Acragas and Syracuse.

IN VICTORY Delphi's Athenian treasury, built after Marathon.

472 The contests of the Olympic Games are now spread over five days. Previously, they had been packed into one day only.

DELPHIC CHARIOTEER An anonymous masterpiece.

468 The young playwright Sophocles enters his first tragedy in the drama competition of Athens' City Dionysia festival – and defeats the well-established playwright Aeschylus.

458-456 The Athenians build the Long Walls, linking Athens with its port, Piraeus.

457 The temple of Zeus is completed at Olympia – one of the most impressive examples of the Doric style in architecture in mainland Greece.

THE REST OF THE WORLD

500 The Carthaginian Hanno sets out with several ships and a large number of would-be colonists to explore the West African coast – possibly reaching as far south as the Senegal river.

496 Battle of Lake Regillus. The Romans defeat the neighbouring Latin peoples, leading to the Cassian Treaty three years later – an alliance with the Latins that will become an important springboard for growing Roman power.

493 The common people (plebeians) of Rome win the right to be represented by their own magistrates, the tribunes. The tribunes will defend the interests of the plebs against

the consuls and Senate.

491 The Babylonian astronomer Naburiannu calculates the length of the lunar month.

486 Xerxes I succeeds his father Darius the Great as King of Persia.

481 In China, a period of acute instability – the so-called era of the Warring States (Chan Kuo) – begins. It will last for more than 250 years.

474 The Greek tyrant Hieron I of Syracuse in Sicily defeats the Etruscans of central Italy in

HIT MAN A Greek archer in the service of an eastern ruler.

the naval battle of Cumae.

465 Palace intrigues at the Persian court result in the assassination of Xerxes I. He is succeeded by his son Artaxerxes I.

458 The Roman Lucius Quinctius Cincinnatus is appointed dictator to save his city from the Aequi people. According to legend, he defeats the enemy in a day and then returns to his life as a simple farmer.

TRIBUTE BEARER A relief from Persepolis, built by Darius I of Persia.

450 – 401 BC

PAID TO ATHENS
A list details tributes paid to Athens by subject states in 440-439.

449 The Persians officially recognise the independence of the Greek city-states in the Peace of Callias.

446 Sparta and Athens agree the Thirty Years Peace – which lasts, in fact, no more than 15 years.

443 The democratic statesman Pericles is elected one of Athens' ten generals, as he will be every year until his death, in 429. His position as the city's leading politician is by now unassailable.

431 Rivalry between Sparta and Athens leads to the outbreak of the Second Peloponnesian War.

421 The Peace of Nicias brings the Second Peloponnesian War to a halt. The fragile truce lasts only six years.

413 An Athenian attempt to conquer Sicily, promoted by the maverick politician Alcibiades, ends in disaster. Troops from Sicily's Greek cities, along with Spartan reinforcements, annihilate the entire Athenian force.

411 The revolution of the Four Hundred imposes oligarchic rule on Athens. But this is replaced the next year with the moderate democratic regime of the Five Thousand.

405 The Spartans, with Persian help, destroy the Athenian fleet at Aegospotami in the Hellespont – spelling the end of Athenian naval supremacy.

404 Spartan troops occupy Athens, bringing the Second Peloponnesian War to an end.

In the aftermath of defeat, the oligarchy of the Thirty is established in Athens. But democratic rule is restored the next year.

The Athenian politician Alcibiades is murdered in exile in Asia Minor, at the instigation of the Spartans.

TRAGEDY The story of Medea inspired Euripides and later dramatists.

431 Euripides' tragedy *Medea* is performed in Athens.

430 Plague breaks out in Athens while besieged by the Spartans. Over the next few years it will carry off a quarter of the city's population – including the statesman Pericles.

Phidias' seated statue of Zeus is installed in the temple of Zeus at Olympia. It will be regarded as one of the Seven Wonders of the Ancient World.

447 Work starts on the Parthenon at Athens.

438 The sculptor Phidias' statue of the goddess Athena is installed in the Parthenon in Athens.

425 Herodotus, author of the first-ever attempt at a systematic historical account (of the Persian wars), dies in the Greek colony of Thurii in southern Italy.

423 The first performance of *The Clouds* by the Athenian comic dramatist Aristophanes. It satirises the teachings of Socrates.

407 Plato joins the circle of Socrates' pupils. He will become one of Socrates' most devoted followers.

IN SEARCH OF TRUTH Socrates' pupil Plato.

---

445 Artaxerxes I of Persia appoints the Israelite Nehemiah governor of Judah. Nehemiah and the priest Ezra will be responsible for rebuilding the walls of Jerusalem and reintroducing to their people the traditional codes and practices of the Judaic Law.

In Rome, the Lex Canuleia allows members of the patrician and plebeian orders to marry one another.

444 Rome occupies the neighbouring city-state of Corioli – an early step in the expansion of its power in Italy.

426 The Romans seize Fidenae, an important river port on the Tiber.

425 Celtic peoples in northern Europe develop the La Tène culture – named after an archaeological site in Switzerland. Their goldsmiths and potters are influenced by work coming from southern Europe but go on to develop their own style with animal and floral designs.

405 The Egyptians rebel against Persian rule.

A declining Persian Empire will not regain control of Egypt for another 60 years.

401 The Battle of Cunaxa. Artaxerxes II of Persia defeats a rebellion led by his younger brother Cyrus. Ten thousand Greek mercenaries fighting for Cyrus escape north to the Black Sea and then home to Greece – an exploit recorded by their leader Xenophon in the *Anabasis*.

IN TROUSERS A priest in the trousers favoured by the Medes and Persians.

400 – 323 BC

AMONG THE GREEKS

395 The Spartan military hero Lysander is killed attacking Haliartus in Boeotia.

386 The 'King's Peace' – after Artaxerxes II of Persia who brokered it – brings the Corinthian War to an end. It leaves Sparta as a weakened but still dominant power in Greece, propped up by Persia.

371 Boeotian victory over the Spartans at the Battle of Leuctra ends a nine-year war between Sparta and an Athenian-Boeotian alliance.

359 The 23-year-old Philip II becomes king of Macedon.

338 The Battle of Chaeroneia. A Greek alliance led by Athens and Thebes is defeated by Philip II of Macedon – marking the beginning of Macedonian dominance in Greece.

336 Philip of Macedon is stabbed by an assassin during the wedding celebrations of his daughter Cleopatra. He is succeeded by his 20-year-old son Alexander.

334 Alexander the Great invades the Persian Empire at the head of a Macedonian-Greek army, defeating Darius III at the Battle of Issus the following year.

327 Having already conquered Asia Minor, Syria, Egypt, Babylonia and Persia, Alexander the Great invades northern India.

323 Alexander the Great dies of a fever at Babylon.

CONQUERING HERO Alexander the Great depicted in a Roman mosaic.

LIFE AND LEARNING

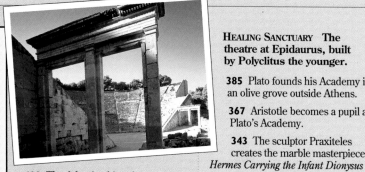

400 The Athenian historian Thucydides dies. His account of the Peloponnesian War is still unfinished.

399 Socrates is condemned to death and executed in Athens, charged with atheism and corrupting the minds of the youth.

The doctor Hippocrates of Cos dies.

HEALING SANCTUARY The theatre at Epidaurus, built by Polyclitus the younger.

385 Plato founds his Academy in an olive grove outside Athens.

367 Aristotle becomes a pupil at Plato's Academy.

343 The sculptor Praxiteles creates the marble masterpiece *Hermes Carrying the Infant Dionysus* for a temple at Olympia.

335 Aristotle founds his school of philosophy, the Lyceum, in a grove outside Athens.

331 Alexander the Great founds the city of Alexandria in Egypt. It will become the largest city of the Greek world and a great centre of learning.

HUNT IN MOSAIC A stag at bay, from Pella in Macedonia.

THE REST OF THE WORLD

396 The growth of Roman power continues as Rome captures the rival city-state of Veii – signalling the end of Etruscan dominance in central Italy.

390 Celtic Gauls from northern Italy sack Rome, and then withdraw. The Romans immediately set about rebuilding the city.

380 The Egyptian general Nectanebo seizes his country's throne, founding the 30th dynasty. This will be Egypt's last native dynasty.

356 Fierce mounted warriors and archers of the nomadic Hsiung-nu people from central Asia threaten northern China. The Chinese build a wall – a forerunner of the Great Wall of China – to try to keep the invaders at bay.

353 Artemisia, widow of Mausolus, ruler of Caria in south-western Asia Minor, starts work on a tomb in honour of her late husband. This is the Mausoleum of Halicarnassus, one of the Seven Wonders of the Ancient World.

343 War breaks out between the Romans and the Samnites of Italy's Adriatic coast.

338 Artaxerxes III of Persia is assassinated by the eunuch Bagoas. Bagoas installs on the Persian throne Artaxerxes' son Arses, who later tries unsuccessfully to get rid of the eunuch by poisoning him. Bagoas then has Arses killed and replaces him on the throne with a relative of the late king who becomes Darius III.

330 Darius III of Persia is assassinated in Bactria in central Asia by a local satrap, Bessus.

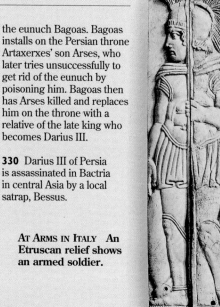

AT ARMS IN ITALY An Etruscan relief shows an armed soldier.

SHIN GUARD The head of a woman ornaments a piece of gold armour from Thrace.

322 A political crisis ushers in the Hellenistic age as Alexander the Great's former generals manoeuvre and fight for control of his empire.

An attempt by Athenian democrats, with allies from other Greek cities, to shake off Macedonian domination is defeated.

301 The Battle of Ipsus in Asia Minor confirms Alexander's former general Ptolemy as ruler of Egypt, while another general Seleucis is left in control of most of Alexander's Asian provinces, which will become the Seleucid Empire. Macedon will fall to the lot of the Antigonid dynasty.

228 Athens obtains its freedom from

ROYAL PROFILES   Ptolemy II of Egypt with his sister-wife.

Macedonian control. As a conservative democracy, it will

remain an impressive cultural centre but with little political influence.

146 The Romans sack Corinth and defeat a Greek army at Leucopetra. Rome now has effective control of the Greek mainland.

66-64 The Roman general Pompey conquers the Hellenistic kingdoms of Asia Minor and Syria, making them provinces of the Roman Empire.

31 The Roman Octavian (later the first Emperor Augustus) defeats Egypt's last Ptolemaic ruler, Cleopatra, at the sea battle of Actium. The Hellenistic world is now firmly under Roman control.

AMONG THE GREEKS

322 The Hellenistic age is marked by the spread of Greek settlers and Greek influence throughout the eastern Mediterranean and Asia Minor.

317 The playwright Menander wins his first victory in Athens' Great Dionysia festival with The Misanthrope. He is a master of the New Comedy style, concerned more with domestic farce than political satire.

306 In Athens, Epicurus founds his school of philosophy.

300 The mathematician Euclid founds his school of

BEAUTY IN STONE
The Venus de Milo.

WORLD WONDERS   Alexandria's lighthouse and a papyrus fragment of a Menander comedy.

geometry in Alexandria in Egypt around this date.

284 The grammarian Zenodotus of Ephesus becomes superintendent of Alexandria's Royal Library.

280 Two of the Seven Wonders of the

Ancient World are constructed around this time: the Pharos (Lighthouse) of Alexandria and the Colossus of Rhodes.

270 The astronomer Aristarchus of Samos, based in Alexandria, puts forward the idea that the Sun lies at the centre of a solar system with the Earth moving round it.

150 An anonymous Greek sculptor from Asia Minor carves a statue of Aphrodite, goddess of love, known to posterity as the *Venus de Milo*.

LIFE AND LEARNING

303 Chandragupta Maurya, ruler of Magadha in northern India, buys the Punjab from Alexander the Great's former general Seleucis I (founder of the Seleucid Empire) for 500 elephants.

272 Asoka, third ruler of the Mauryan dynasty, begins a 37-year reign. Under him the Mauryan Empire will include all but the southern tip of the Indian subcontinent.

264-241 The First Punic War between Rome and Carthage ends in defeat for Carthage.

218 The Carthaginian general Hannibal crosses the Alps from southern Gaul into Italy at the start of

the Second Punic War. He defeats the Romans at Trasimene and Cannae.

202 The Roman general Scipio defeats Hannibal and the Carthaginians at Zama. The Second Punic War ends with Carthaginian surrender the next year.

164 The Jewish leader Judas Maccabeus captures Jerusalem. He rededicates the Temple which the previous Seleucid rulers had desecrated in an attempt to impose Greek religion on the Jews.

149-146 The Third Punic War ends with

the Roman sack of Carthage. The city is razed to the ground, dedicated to the infernal gods and human habitation forbidden there.

55 Julius Caesar invades Britain.

44 Julius Caesar, recently appointed dictator for life, is assassinated.

42 Battle of Philippi. Julius Caesar's nephew Octavian and friend Mark Antony defeat Brutus and Cassius who had taken part in Caesar's assassination.

37 Herod the Great becomes King of Judea.

COIN FROM CARTHAGE
Hannibal invaded Italy using elephants.

THE REST OF THE WORLD

INDEX

ACKNOWLEDGMENTS

ABBREVIATIONS
T = Top; M = Middle; B = Bottom;
R = Right; L = Left

AKG = Archiv für Kunst und Geschichte, London
BPK = Bildarchiv Preussischer Kulturbesitz, Berlin
BM = British Museum, London
CI = Christie's Images, London
EL = Erich Lessing
ETA = E.T. Archive, London
GDO = G. Dagli Orti, Paris
HF = Hirmer Fotoarchiv, Munich
KHV = Kunsthistorisches Museum, Vienna
MMA = Metropolitan Museum of Art, New York
MNN = Museo Nazionale, Naples
ML = Musée du Louvre, Paris
NMA = National Museum, Athens
SAM = Stäaliche Antiksammlungen, Munich
SMB = Stäatliche Museen, Berlin
TBA = Toucan Books Archive, London

1 Apollo, Delphi Museum/TBA. 2-3 MMA, gift of Walter G. Baker, 1956. 4 Horse and jockey, NMA/GDO, TL; Javelin thrower, SMB/BPK, TR; Wrestlers, *c*510 BC, NMA/GDO, B. 5 Vase, detail of Hera, 470 BC, SAM/AKG/EL, TL; Bronze mirror, 460 BC, Canellopolos Museum, Athens/GDO, TR; Corinth, Tony Stone Images/Charlie Waite, ML; Amphora of a girl on a swing (ref: F60), 430-420 BC, ML/TBA, BL; Statuette of a girl, 1st century BC, ML/AKG/EL, BR. 6 Dolphin fresco, Knossos, 1450-1400 BC, Michael Holford. 7 Cephalonia, Robert Harding Picture Library/G. Kavallierakis. 8-9 Map by Nick Skelton. 10 Vase, detail of Hephaistos, 525 BC, KHV/AKG/EL. 11 Minoan bull's head, Archaeological Museum, Heraklion/AKG/EL. 12-13 *The Tribute of Keftiu, Keta and Tunip*, copy of an Egyptian tomb painting by N. de Garis Davies, BM. 14-15 Illustration by Terence Dalley. 16 Mosaic, detail from Pompeii, AKG/EL, T; Athens, 1830, by Edward Dodwell, AKG/EL, B. 17 Votive relief of a family offering a ram to Dionysus, ML/AKG/EL. 18 Pyxis of the birth of Athena (ref: CA 616), 570-560 BC, ML/TBA. 19 Vase, detail of soldiers, 6th century BC, NMA/GDO; 20 Corinthian funeral hydria (ref: E643), ML/TBA. 21 Detail of Artemis from the Parthenon Frieze, Acropolis Museum, Athens/AKG/EL. 22 Detail from vase (ref: E69), BM. 23 Detail from a pyxis of a wedding scene (ref: B1447), BM, T; Wedding vase, 5th century BC, ML/AKG/EL, B. 24 Vase, detail, *c*450 BC, NMA/TBA. 25 Grave stele (ref: MS 5470), University of Pennsylvania Museum, Philadelphia, T; Detail of Oinochoe (ref: F596), *c*490 BC, BM, B. 26 Nurse and Baby, Museo di Cipro, Nicosia/AKG/EL, T; Illustration by Gill Tomblin, B. 27 Illustration by Gill Tomblin, T; Baby's bottle, BM, B. 28 Marble grave relief, MMA, Fletcher Fund, 1927. 30 Marble relief of boy with a hoop, 4th century BC, NMA/TBA, TL; Toys, BM/TBA, TR. 31 Detail of kylix of boy fishing (ref: 01.8024), 480 BC, Boston Museum of Fine Arts, H.L. Pierce Fund, T; Vase, detail of woman juggling, TBA, B. 32 Archaic relief of dancing girls, Acropolis Museum, Athens/GDO, T; Terracotta figurine (ref: G. 577), Hermitage Museum, St Petersburg/TBA, B. 33 Vase, detail of athletes (ref: G.7), ML/TBA. 34 Detail of Attic jug, SMB/TBA. 35 Homer, TBA. 36-37 Illustration by Gill Tomblin. 38 Detail of bowl, *c*500 BC, SMB/TBA. 39 Detail of bowl showing schooling, 480 BC, SMB/BPK/Johannes Laurentius, T; Detail of Attic 86 Amphora with Athena, *c*480 BC, SMB/TBA, B. 40 Grave relief 873, 4th century BC, NMA/TBA, T; Vase, detail of an athlete, 6th century BC, Musée Vivenel, Compiègne/AKG/EL, B. 41 Relief of cat and dog baiting, *c*510 BC, NMA/TBA. 42 Detail of vase (ref: E270), BM. 43 Socrates, bust, 4th century BC, AKG/EL. 44-45 Illustration by Gill Tomblin. 45 Detail of bowl, National Museum, Copenhagen/TBA. 46 Calyx krater of the dead Sarpendon carried by Thanatos and Hypnos, *c*515 BC, MMA, purchase, gift of Darius Ogden Mills, gift of J. Pierpont Morgan, and bequest of Joseph H. Durkee, by exchange, 1972. 47 Illustration by Gill Tomblin. 48 Bronze mask, Archaeological Museum, Piraeus, T. 49 Detail from a drinking cup (ref: GR 1893.3-3.1), BM/TBA. 50 Bronze Statue (ref: GR 1865.7-12.1 Bronze 848), BM. 51 Mosaic, MNN/Scala. 52 Vase, detail of Heracles killing his lyre teacher (ref: 2646), SAM/Studio Koppermann, T; Vase stand showing revellers (ref: GR 1842 4-7,14), BM, B. 53 Odysseus and Penelope, terracotta relief, 460-450 BC, ML/AKG/EL. 54 Pottery fragment of mourning figure (ref: Gr 1931.1-14.5), 340 BC, BM, T; Illustration by Gill Tomblin, B. 55 Vase, detail of funerary rites, 6th century BC, NMA/GDO. 56 Funerary necklace (ref: Gr 1953. 4-14.1), *c*350 BC, BM, T; Loutrophos, ML, B. 57 Attic grave relief, TBA. 58 Demeter, Triptolemos and Persephone, marble relief, 430-420 BC, NMA/AKG/EL, T; Detail of Hydria showing Cerberus (ref: E701), *c*525 BC, ML/TBA, B. 59 Detail of Attic vase with servants carrying plates, 4th century BC, NMA/GDO. 60 Illustration by Gill Tomblin. 61 Acropolis, Athens, AKG/EL. 62 Detail from Attic Lecythos showing hunter, 500 BC, KHV/AKG/EL, T; African slave, BM/Michael Holford, B. 63-64 Illustration by Gill Tomblin. 65 Detail of Parthenon frieze, BM/Michael Holford, T; Athenian coin, TBA, B. 66 Terracotta figure of woman on mule, AKG, T; Illustration by Gill Tomblin, B. 67 Shoemakers, detail of Attic vase, *c*450 BC, Mansell Collection. 68-69 Illustration by Gill Tomblin. 70 Vase detail of women at well, TBA. 71 Amphora, detail of men weighing merchandise (ref: 47.11.5), MMA, purchase, Joseph Pulitzer Bequest, 1947, T; Official grain measure, Agora Museum, Athens/GDO, BL; Official measure for liquids, Agora Museum, Athens/GDO, BR. 72 Hydria (ref: Gr 1885 12-13-18, vase E190), BM. 73 Illustration by Gill Tomblin. 74 Drawing from a vase of women working wool (ref: 31.11.10), 6th century BC, MMA, Fletcher Fund, 1931, T; Terracotta Onos, ML/GDO, B. 75 Relief of woman using a chest for storage, HF. 76 Illustration by Gill Tomblin. 77 Oil Lamp (ref: Gr 1913 11-14.1), BM. 78 Rhyton (ref: Gr 1867-8.1289, F 433), BM, T; Illustration by Gill Tomblin, B. 79 Wall painting from Paestum, AKG/EL. 80 Fish plate (ref: Gr 1876, 11-121), BM. 81 Attic pot, 5th century BC, Château Musée, Boulogne-sur-Mer/AKG/EL, T; Bronze cooking utensils, 6th century BC, CI, B. 82 Detail of vase showing athlete using a strigil, 5th century BC, KMV/AKG/EL, T; Bronze strigil (ref: B320), Musée Royal de Mariemont, Morlanweltz/TBA, B. 83 Detail of drinking cup, *c*500 BC, MMA/Claus Hansmann, Munich, T; Oil container, *c*575-550 BC, Musée Royal de Mariemont, Morlanweltz/TBA, B. 84 Marble korai, 6th century BC, Acropolis Museum, Athens/GDO, T; Gem portrait in jasper of bearded man, 5th century BC, Boston Museum of Fine Arts, Francis Bartlett Fund, B. 85 Vase (ref: F164), BM, T; Four scent jars (refs: 1658,1660,1631,1641), BM, B. 86 Illustration by Gill Tomblin, T; Bronze figure, CI, B. 87 Illustration by Gill Tomblin. 88 Cup, detail of man with hat, 510 BC, SAM/TBA, T; Girl tying sandal, SMB/BPK, B. 89 Interior of Cup (ref: F68), ML/TBA. 90-91 Spartan Plain, Ekdotike Athenon, Athens. 91 Spartan warrior, Ancient Art and Architecture Collection, London. 92 Democracy relief, TBA. 93 Pericles, BM, T; Ostrakon, Agora Museum, Athens, B. 94-95 Illustration by Gill Tomblin. 95 Tokens, Agora Museum, Athens/TBA. 96 Water clock, Agora Museum, Athens/TBA. 97 Illustration by Gill Tomblin, T; Juror's ballots, Agora Museum, Athens/TBA, B. 98 Greek soldiers, *c*560-550 BC, ML/AKG/EL. 99 Vase, detail of council of war, MNN/TBA. 100 Bronze cavalry officer (ref: 904 7-3), 550 BC, BM. 101 Illustration by Gill Tomblin, T; Vase, detail of Thracian woman, SAM/TBA; Tririme relief, C.M. Dixon, T; Reconstructed tririme in Greek navy, Tririme Trust, University of Cambridge/Paul Lifke, B. 104 Silver Ram (ref: Silver 58), BM. 105 Olive Grove, Naxos, Robert Harding Picture Library. 106 Archaic terracotta figurine, ML/GDO. 107 Attic amphora, detail of Olive Gathering, BM/TBA, T; Terracotta relief of olive press (ref: D 550), BM, B. 108 Vase, detail of artist painting statue of Heracles (ref: 50.11.4, Side 1), MMA, T. 109 Illustration by Gill Tomblin, T; Vase, detail of carpenter (ref: Vase E23), BM, B; Vase, detail of bronzesmiths at work, BPK. 111 Hellenistic gold necklace and earrings, CI, T; Hellenistic silver bowls, 4th century BC, CI, B. 112 Coins, TBA. 112-13 Illustration by Gill Tomblin. 113 Vase in form of African's head, 6th century BC, NMA/TBA, B. 114 Ethiopian warrior, C.M. Dixon, T; Master and slave, National Museum, Copenhagen/TBA. 116 Lyre (ref: 1816. 6 -10 50 1), BM, T; Terracotta figurine of girl with flute, ML/AKG/EL, B. 117 Vase, detail of Satyr chorus (ref: E768), BM, T; Terracotta figurine of girl with zither, ML/AKG/EL, B. 118 Theatre at Dodona, C.M. Dixon, T; Illustration by Gill Tomblin, B. 119 Actor with mask, Photothèque André Held, Ecublens. 120 Detail of scene from *The Oresteia*, by Aeschylus, Museo Archeologico, Ferrara, HF, T; Drunken figures, ML/AKG/EL, B. 121 Vase, detail from *The Knights*, by Aristophanes, SMB/BPK, L; Masks, National Museum, Copenhagen/TBA, TR, MR, BR. 122 Spartan girl athlete (ref: Bronze 208), BM, T; Detail of boxers (ref: B 607), BM. 123 Diver, Museo Archeologico, Paestum/AKG/EL. 124 Vase, detail of athletes jumping (ref: B418), BM, T; Jumping weights, 6th-5th century BC, NMA/TBA, BL; Panathenaic amphora of chariot race (ref: 4595), Museo Archeologico Nazionale, Taranto/TBA, BR. 125 Vase, detail of athlete with victory ribbons, 520-510 BC, SMB/BPK. 126 Winner with prize tripod, National Museum, Copenhagen/TBA, T; Victory wreaths, Private Collection, Amsterdam/TBA, B. 127 Sacrifice to Persephone, Museo Archeological, Taranto/Scala. 128 Early gods, Cyprus Medelhausmuseet, Stockholm/Margareta Sjöblom. 129 Apotheosis of Homer, *c*200 BC, BM, T; Vase, detail of altar offering, ML/AKG/EL, B. 130 Detail of Parthenon frieze, Acropolis Museum, Athens/Scala. 132 Mount Olympus, AKG/EL. 133 Bronze head of Zeus, 490 BC, NMA/AKG/EL, T; Boreas abducting Oreithyia, detail of Oehochoë (ref: K35), *c*36 BC, ML/TBA, B. 134 Illustration by Gill Tomblin. 136 Bronze figure of a man praying, SMB/TBA, T; Temple of Segesta, Sicily, 5th century BC, AKG/EL, B. 137 Religious procession, Museo Archeological, Ferrara/Scala. 138 Dionysiac orgy, Scala, T; Dionysus cup, *c*530 BC (ref: F144), ML/TBA, B. 139 Satyr on a gilded bronze vessel, late 4th century BC, Archaeological Museum, Thessaloniki/TBA. 140 Delphi, Zefa Photos. 141 Oracle from Dodona, C.M. Dixon, T; Vase, detail of Delphic Oracle, SMB/BPK, B. 142 Votive relief, 4th century BC, NMA/AKG/EL. 143 Marble relief of foot, TBA. 144 Relief of doctor and child (ref: Sculpture 629), BM, T; Bust of Hippocrates, TBA, B. 145 Medical instruments, BM/TBA, T; Vase, detail of Achilles binding Patroclus' wound, 5th century BC, SMB/BPK, B. 146 Metrological relief (ref: Micxh813), Ashmolean Museum, Oxford. 147 Mosaic of the death of Archimedes, Liebighaus, Frankfurt-am-Main/AKG/EL, T; Papyrus fragment, Cornell University/TBA, B. 149 *Pheidias and the Frieze of the Parthenon, Athens,* oil painting by L. Alma-Tadema, Birmingham Museums and Art Gallery. 150 Minoan double-headed axe, 1700-1600 BC, Archaeological Museum, Heraklion/AKG/EL, TL; Trojan horse, *c*670 BC, Mykonos Museum/AKG/EL, ML; Ramses III, AKG/EL, B. 151 Spartan cup, Bibliothèque Nationale, Paris/TBA, ML; Aristogeiton, NMA/Mansell Collection, TR; Geometric pyxis, ML/TBA, ML; Sappho, MNN/AKG/EL, MR; Babylonian statue at Zenjirli, TBA, BL; Tiled relief of Babylonian lion, ML/AKG/EL, BR. 152 Hoplites, Musée Chatillieu-sur-Seine/Giraudon, TL; Thermistocles, TBA, TR; Treasury House, Delphi, AKG/EL, ML; Delphic charioteer, 470 BC, MR; Relief form Persepolis, TBA, BL; Vase, detail of mercenary (ref: E 135), BM, BL. 153 Fragment of Athenian tribute list for the year 440-439 BC, TBA, TL; Scene from Medea, by Euripedes, Mansell Collection, ML; Plato, TBA, MR; Persian figure from the Oxus treasure, BM, B. 154 Phillip II, Bibliothèque Nationale, Paris/AKG/EL, TL; Alexander the Great, MNN/AKG/EL, TR; Theatre at Epidaurus, GDO, ML; Fresco from Pompeii, AKG/EL, MR; Thracian figure, Regional Museum of History, Vraca, Bulgaria/AKG/EL, BL; Latin soldiers, Villa Guilia, Rome/Mansell Collection, BR. 155 Ptolomy II, KMV/AKG/EL, T; Venus de Milo, 1st century BC, ML/Giraudon, ML; Engraving of the lighthouse at Alexandria, AKG/EL, ML; Script of play by Menander, TBA, MR; Silver coin, BM, B.

Front cover: Illustration by Gill Tomblin, TL; Metropolitan Museum of Art, New York, Fletcher Fund, 1927, detail, ML; Zefa Photos, MM; Metropolitan Museum of Art, New York, Claus Hausmann, Munich, MR; AKG/Erich Lessing, BL; Christies Images, MM; BM; BR.

Back cover: ADG/Erich Lessing, TL; ML; MR; SMB/BPK, BL; Illustration by Gill Tomblin, BR.

The editors are grateful to the following individuals and publishers for their kind permission to quote passages from the books below:
Batsford Ltd from *Everyday Life in Ancient Greece* by Marjorie and C.H.B. Quennell, revised by Kathleen Freeman, 1954.
Cambridge University Press from *The World of Athens: An Introduction to Classical Athenian Culture,* edited by the Joint Association of Classical Teachers, 1984.
Constable & Co Ltd from *Sexual Life in Ancient Greece* by Hans Licht, translated by J.H. Freese and edited by Lawrence H. Dawson, 1994.
Cornell University Press from *The Greek Way of Life: From Conception to Old Age* by Robert Garland, 1990.
Methuen & Co Ltd from *A History of Greece* by Cyril E. Robinson, 1966.
Prospect Books from *Life of Luxury: Europe's Oldest Cookery Book* by Archestratus, translated by John Wilkins and Sean Hill, 1994.
Stamford Hill Stationers Ltd from *Athenian Politics: Democracy in Athens from Pericles to Cleophon,* edited by the London Association of Classical Teachers.
Weidenfeld & Nicolson from *Daily Life in Greece at the Time of Pericles* by Robert Flaceliere, translated by Peter Green, 1965.